THE MICK-RICK DEBATES

For my friend +
Colleague, Dave James
with great respect +
affection
Dick DeBlume

THE MICK-RICK DEBATES

Controversies in Contemporary Christianity

Michael Maasdorp and Richard Arthur DeRemee

To order additional copies of this book, contact:
Xlibris Corporation
1-888-795-4274
www.Xlibris.com
Orders@Xlibris.com
38405

CONTENTS

DEDICATION

For Michael:

"To John Fremlin and other exiles"

For Richard:

"To my grandchildren, Sten, Roland, Clara, Arthur, Catherine, Ian and Nils"

Foreword from Michael (Mick)

Some thirty years ago I celebrated the Eucharist for the last time. It was a sad moment as I wondered what the future held for my ministry as an ordained person. I took some comfort, however, in the thought that when life is given a chance, it always prevails. Only many years later did I discover that I could validly equate this transforming "life" with the "God" of traditional Christian teaching.

During my continuing exile from the Christian fold I have evolved an understanding of Jesus which does not depend upon belonging to the institutional Church.

First, I have discovered that there is more loving care outside the Church than within it. The conviction of many Church people that they have ultimate answers to at least some of life's mysteries seems to preclude an entire range of behavioral options.

Second, it gradually came to me that I wasn't missing either worship or prayer—those two basic staple foods of the so-called Christian life (God). If that was the case, why bother with either in their traditional form?

Third, and most important, I was at last forced to acknowledge that everything I was experiencing indicated that I can know God (life) only through this world. The super-natural realm which I had always assumed lies "behind" this natural reality turned out to have been a mistake.

Living out a non-religious Christianity has over the years brought some bleak moments. But there have been many more starbursts of insight and joy. One of these was an E-mail out of the cyberspace blue from Richard DeRemee—the "Rick" of these debates. From our first tentative explorations eventually arose the idea that he and I might collaborate in writing about our differing experiences of being Christian. This we have done for the past two years or so.

Perhaps our debates will prove useful to those many for whom life (God) is an exciting progress of joyous if sometimes painful discovery and renewal—as contrasted with the bitter rearguard struggle of so many traditional Christians to hold doctrinal palisades against the predations of secular anti-Christs.

Foreword from Richard (Rick)

It is interesting and important to note that without the Internet and E-mail this series of debates would not have occurred. In the fall of 2004 while surfing the Net in search of interesting sites related to my passions of religion and philosophy I came upon the "Radical Faith" web site. It is the site maintained by my interlocutor, Michael. I was attracted by the challenges it cast in the face of my traditional beliefs. Frankly I was a bit upset by what was said concerning these beliefs. The heat of my indignation galvanized me to send an E-mail asking if it would be possible to contribute some of my opinions regarding the issues discussed on the site.

After Michael read some of my writings, I took his "fog index" test, passed muster and gained admission to his inner sanctum. The debates began. This was one of the most rewarding opportunities I was ever offered and I am exceedingly grateful to Michael.

For two years we alternately proposed one word subjects and went back and forth on the Internet until we felt enough was said. Often we agreed to disagree but we were always civil and respectful. Many times we found common ground that usually rested at the feet of Jesus Christ. We were on separate roads to the same city. Although the roads were sometimes difficult to navigate, we both enjoyed our journeys immensely.

Lest my conservative friends think I lost my way and abjured my long-held faith anchored in the traditions of the Evangelical Lutheran Church in America (ELCA), I assure them I have not. If anything, my faith is strengthened, thanks to answering in my mind the penetrating challenges posed by my friend, Michael.

I came to realize through these debates that faith unexamined may be at risk. I needed to repeatedly ask myself why I believed in so and so and how I believed this in the light of science and the modern world in general. Now I have come through the test of fire, not unchanged, but with a greater understanding of the nature of faith and how it can evolve in a changing world.

Modernity should not destroy our religious traditions. Challenges to them ought to cause us to search deeply to find the nuggets of durable and immutable truths buried therein so we can translate and express them in our modern vernaculars.

While we may coalesce around commonly-shared beliefs bringing us into fellowship with an organized church, it seems to me every individual is free to see God and His creation in the light of his or her unique experiences and traditions. Hopefully this will help us to re-examine our prejudices and short comings and guide us all on the path to a more peaceful, fruitful and rewarding world.

1

Survival

The Church preaches about how we're supposed to live. One of the most important directives is the "Love God, love your neighbor" rule. But does it make sense? What about the everyday struggle to survive?

Mick: As you know, Rick, I'm deeply concerned that the Church is failing to bring Jesus of Nazareth into the 21st century. One of my gripes is that traditional theology *if taken seriously* makes ordinary life impossible for Christians. That's why so few today want anything to do with Jesus.

I refer in particular to the need to survive. Survival requires each of us to compete to live. Sometimes we have to kill or be killed. The weak go the wall—though, once they're there, Christians are encouraged to be kind to them.

I have never come across an official Christian doctrine about day-to-day survival. It is as though we are expected to live in two worlds. One is secular, where we live normally. The other is religious, where we are holy.

The Church's central message, if I understand correctly, is that we should "Love God with everything we've got, and others as we love ourselves" (Mark 12.-29-31). Now, anyone who has ever been in business (or war) knows all-too-well that this not only doesn't, but cannot work.

In other words, this important rule for being a "good" Christian is full of holes. What do you make of it?

Rick: The issues you raise impinge on the basic questions, "Is human life meaningful, does it have purpose and can we obtain happiness in this life?" If the answer is yes, how can we bring this about?

I believe that the life and message of Jesus of Nazareth provide a critical guide in this quest.

What is meant by survival? Perhaps it means personal success on a physical, economic or prestige level, derived at the expense of others. If so, we are talking about a Darwinian animal-world, not one made up of conscious, rational humans who have the capacity for moral action.

If the principle of "love your neighbor" is no longer relevant how are we different from animals and what other principle could supplant it?

Competition cannot and should not be eliminated. It is a fundamental human quality. If leavened by moral responsibility it can be a force for good. To be sure, we have not yet achieved perfection. We wage war and kill, we cheat, we dominate, we do not love.

These imperfections used to be included under the rubric of sin. How do we bring these faults and imperfections to a conscious level so we can take effective remedial measures?

Mick: I'm not going to be side-tracked into discussing sin. That way there be dragons. Let's stay with survival.

I agree that competition is a "fundamental human quality". But aren't you still avoiding reality? It doesn't make sense to step aside for those who are less able than me. Even in the sacred sanctuaries of the Church, clergy compete for power like anyone else. They preach "love your neighbor"—but nevertheless strive to be top-dog.

A just society is one where the playing field is as level as possible. I admit that there should be social equity. But not equality. If I'm fitter, I am right to shoulder the less-fit aside. That's the way God made the world, as the whole of nature witnesses. We *are* animals, set apart only by superior intelligence. The latter does not liberate us from the demands of survival, though it does give us an advantage over other animals.

I maintain that the old Hebrew "Love your neighbor" rule reiterated by Jesus has to be understood anew. If not, it must be dismissed as nonsense.

Rick: About 50 years ago, one of my professors of philosophy gave a talk about Christian love. He pointed to colleagues in the audience and said there were some he didn't like—but that he loved them all. He distinguished personal affection from the need to treat his fellow humans with concern and justice. Maybe the meaning of the word "love" is a sticking point.

When we compete, as we often must, we should be mindful of this principle. If love and affection occur together it's wonderful. It is not disaster when they don't coincide.

The "Love your neighbor" rule is already dismissed by many as nonsense. But that hardly justifies abandoning it. Maybe distinguishing love from affection will help some to survive competition with a sense of integrity.

Mick: Perhaps we're getting somewhere. I want to take up two points.

First, may I test you on the phrase "Christian love"? It seems to me that love is just love. There is nothing specially Christian about it. People love whether or not they are Christian. Love is independent of the Church. Jesus didn't invent love. It wasn't absent before his birth and somehow present afterwards.

Second, I maintain that love and survival are complimentary. It's not true that when we love others we're good and that we're bad when we do what we must to survive. Those who love best, survive best. To survive best, it is best to love well.

Your philosophy professor presumably knew that. After all he was a professor. He was paid more; had greater prestige and power; like the Centurion he was able to tell others to come and go. I bet he knew that some listening to him would have taken his job with hardly a backward glance.

But to advance a little. Are you equating "love" with "concern and justice"?

Rick: Christians do not have a corner on love nor does any religion. Each religion lives on different flanks of the same great mountain called God. Each sees the mountain from an individual perspective. All contemplate the same mountain. As individuals we reside on one side of the mountain by accident of birth or circumstance. Choice may move one from one side to another. Hence, when I speak of "Christian love" I refer to the version exemplified by the life of Christ. That is my particular view of that great mountain. It is the light I was handed to illuminate my particular path through darkness.

Language is often weak and ineffective in defining concepts such as love. I include "concern and justice". But descriptors such as clemency and patience are among many possible others. Love is a state of mind. It shapes our actions toward others. It maximizes the possibilities of fruitful life and happiness, not only for the loved but for the lover as well.

I don't think that showing love necessarily results in a good outcome. By proffering love we are not buying an indulgence. If our motive for giving love is to manipulate others for our own advantage it is no longer love.

As for my professor, from the perspective of 50 years I think he would chuckle at the idea he was exercising power or prestige or that anyone would want his meagerly-salaried position.

Mick: Do I understand you properly, Rick?

- The need to survive is indeed a fact of life.
- Jesus of Nazareth lived a loving life.
- Christians follow Jesus. So they also should love others.
- Love is a state of mind. It shapes how we behave.
- It issues in concern, justice, clemency, patience and other good behaviors.
- It excludes manipulation for personal advantage such as survival.
- Love may not lead to a "good outcome".

With reservations, I think I can go along with you up to the final point. Will you explain what you mean by it, please?

Rick: Yes, Mick, you have fairly represented my position. Implicit in my previous remarks are the criteria by which I would judge the "outcomes" of love. I begin by excluding love exercised for personal gain. It is not the kind of love demonstrated by Christ. To reiterate, love is fundamentally a state of mind geared to ". . . maximize the possibilities of fruitful life and happiness, not only for the loved but for the lover as well."

The love equation is first and foremost composed of two persons, the lover and the loved. For the equation to be balanced, the lover must be genuine, selfless and with pure intention. The loved should demonstrate evidence of the effect, namely a fruitful and happy life. It is this binary relationship of two persons that constitutes the cells of which other bodies are made such as society, churches and complex organizations.

If the lover is unsuccessful in eliciting the hoped-for result, solace may still be found in having fought the good fight, finished the race and kept the faith.

In closing I once more cite the example of Christ. He is the genuine lover. But many of the loved have not responded.

Mick: Fair enough. Now, you'll recall that I wondered why the Church has no doctrine of survival. It does teach about "love" and I wondered if survival and love are compatible.

I think we agree at one level. Goodwill as a "state of mind" must precede loving action, both interpersonal and social. The latter application of love we call "justice".

At another level I sense we differ radically. Yes, love must be generous, giving, caring, clement, patient and so on. But just producing at list of loving actions will not do. What of the exceptions?

Maximizing life requires hard choices.

In war it may be right to decimate one city to save two. Cutting jobs to overcome or contain competition may be a just action in business. A marriage may be rightly broken to save children. Murder may be right to keep others alive. It may be right to take a professorship at the expense of the less-competent. It might even be life-giving to give your life ("commit suicide").

I say that we love when we first calculate and then take the most life-giving action. Augustine of Hippo wrote: "*Dilige et quod vis, fac*". That is, "Take loving care—and then what you decide, do." So provided I have goodwill, and when I have weighed up the options as best I can, *whatever* I choose is loving and therefore right.

That is also most likely to result in individual and corporate survival.

Rick: Your thoughts bring to mind words of Dietrich Bonhoeffer:

"It is worse to be evil than to do evil."

The quality of moral action and the responsibility for it finally resides with the individual. Moral decisions ought not be the result of going down a check list but should be tailored to fit the real-time circumstance. A survival plan or plan for living cannot be formulated into a stagnant doctrine with check lists, just as love cannot be.

I find an analogy in my experience as a physician.

After a long and pedantic education I was abruptly sent out to treat patients. My encounters were never structured and clear cut. I was expected to act appropriately and get a good result for the patient. Although I had been given many facts and check lists to follow, they were for the most part in the subconscious as I acted intuitively in real time. I was given immense freedom of action by the public I served, with their implicit understanding I possessed sufficient knowledge and *character* for the task.

Is it not similar in our daily lives?

Through our learning and nurture as children we develop our personalities and character. Hopefully we are mature by the time we are cut loose to survive. With fingers crossed we hope to meet each moral and survival challenge as it arises in a manner consistent with our character. The only standard to be applied in our decisions is the example of Christ.

2

Progress

Rick: Creating change is a prime characteristic of conscious human beings. In fact, creating change could be considered a test for consciousness. Progress implies change but change does not always indicate progress.

Evidence of change is in abundance in modern society. Businessmen and leaders of all sorts admonish their employees to adapt to change and continuously seek it. It is decidedly unpopular to look backward. Change is frequently sought for its own sake with little or no thought given to the possible outcomes. This preoccupation with change seems to have accelerated during the economic boom of the past 50 years.

Here is my question to you, Mick: Has human society made any progress?

Mick: I could respond, "It depends what you mean by progress." But I don't like to cavil.

"Society" is a concept too large for me to deal with directly. So let me use an image. Picture an ordinary person like you or me. We begin as tiny cells which multiply into a baby. We grow, changing all the time. As you and I know all-too-well change continues apace even into old age. The final change is death.

We normally think of a person developing fast into early adulthood. But is it not true that the changes of old age are also development?

The question is this: Do we progress as we develop? Perhaps in this context development and progression are synonyms. Or is it better to think of regression after a certain point in the human life cycle?

If this image has any force, is societal change development or progress? I looked up Robert Browning's answer:

> Progress, man's distinctive mark alone,
> Not God's, and not the beasts': God is, they are,
> Man partly is and wholly hopes to be.

Rick: I must define "progress" to be sure we are discussing the same thing.

> Progress implies continuous improvement or movement toward betterment and a higher more advanced stage.

As I grow older, my body is deteriorating. Fortunately I don't think my mind is. I can say I have progressed in my appreciation and understanding of life. So in applying the definition of "progress" to anything, we have to be particular about what we are judging.

It is popular in some circles to talk of "human progress" as though it were a given. In the area of science and technology a case can certainly be made for progress. Then again, much suffering and need could have been ameliorated by those disciplines, but hasn't.

Progress has not occurred on all fronts. Humanity has often failed to use the intelligence and tools it has been given. This reality raises a question. Are we really any better than our brethren of classical Greece, or of Palestine at the rise of Christ?

I am trying to be particular about what we are judging. I submit that moral character is the most important aspect of humanity. Have we made progress in that dimension?

Mick: I rest easy with what you say about progress in general. Like you, I don't support those who are uncritical about it. Utopians delude themselves.

You are concerned with moral progress. This question is typical of Christians. It derives in part from a flawed construct:

1. The human race is intrinsically corrupt; and
2. This corruption is passed from generation to generation.

The account of the "Fall" in the Bible is still taught by many as something which actually happened. Others say it is a myth which helps us understand how things really are. Yet others say it's merely an interesting story which tells us how the first Hebrews understood the world. But the assumption that we are all sinful is a given.

My question concerning moral progress is different. I ask, "Given evolution and genetics, in what sense do human beings do wrong?" Only when that is answered can we revert to your question about moral progress. What do you think?

Rick: I have a somewhat different construct.

1. Humans have the potential for both good and bad.
2. These characteristics are passed from generation to generation by both somatic genes and by culture and tradition or what might be considered "cultural DNA".

Evolution has crowned us with consciousness making us radically different than animals. Consciousness thrusts moral decisions on us and gives us the tools for rational thought to act for good or ill. When I read the newspaper or view television, all the ways that humans do wrong is painfully apparent.

I am not sure that humans have made or will ever make "progress" on the moral front. Perhaps that is why we seek something beyond the material world. Our nature has not sufficiently evolved to always make good moral decisions. Therefore, if we have any possibility of finding meaningfulness in our individual lives and for society at large, there must be a standard of good to which we can look for guidance beyond this material existence. Could it be that morality is a factor in natural selection? Could it be that questions of morality do not lend themselves to the test of progress? That is to say, the bedrock of morality is firm and unchangeable and it is only the extent of the exercise of moral action that can be judged for progress?

Mick: Hooray! I think we agree—up to a point.

To summarize:

- Humans are the product of nature (genes and so on) and nurture ("cultural DNA").
- We are aware of a moral dimension to our lives.

The question now is: From where are moral standards derived. I can't know "black" unless I also know "white". Similarly, the notion of "wrong" requires that I know what is "right".

How we deal with life changes from age to age. Some call this progress. I think it is just cultural mutation to cope with new and recurring challenges.

In contrast, the pace of physical change in humans is extremely slow. We are now just as we were 50 000 or more years ago. That is, human needs and functions remain constant, while natural and social environments change relatively fast. So it only *seems* as though there is moral bedrock.

If this approach is valid, I conclude that we *choose* right and wrong. You seem to disagree, talking of moral guidance from "beyond the material". What do you mean by that?

Rick: There *is* moral bedrock. It is expressed, not as a trivial list of does and don'ts, but as a set of areas or categories of moral concern. These concerns have confronted human kind since the dawn of rational consciousness. They are:

1. Concern for human life
2. Concern for individual dignity
3. Concern for personal identity and integrity
4. Concern for one's neighbor and society
5. Concern for the significance of human existence

These concerns serve as templates for each generation to lay over its peculiar circumstances. They are prescriptive only in the sense they are inscribed in human nature and cannot be avoided. Not only have human needs and functions remained constant, so have the categories of concern. How these categories are interpreted is up to each society and individual. Differences and nuances will be shaped by individual traditions and experience. Who can say what is correct? That does not mean that each person cannot have their own beliefs and interpretations.

Are these categories "beyond material", the work of an intelligent creator, or simply the result of chance material evolution? I cannot say which view is absolute truth, nor do I think anyone can. Nevertheless, I retain my own personal answer to the question. It is a matter of *choice.* I respect anyone's belief system as long as it does not deprive me of my own choices.

Mick: Perhaps we agree. Let me test that with this summary.

Each of us makes a personal choice of a moral bedrock. We try to choose that bedrock sensibly—usually from a combination of social options and our own life experiences. But there is no way of knowing if the bedrock each chooses has absolute validity (that is, "comes from God", to use ancient parlance).

I have little doubt that as a person I have made progress in some ways over the years. And from the little I know of history, it seems that human societies have progressed in some respects over many millennia. But because human evolution is so slow, I can't say that our *nature* has progressed in the same sense. Therefore, the moral choices most of us have to make today differ from the past in context but not in essence.

Rick: I agree, Mick. It may well be that moral choice is the key to long term survival and progress of humanity.

I cannot escape the idea that moral choice is embedded in our physical nature. Our brain could be compared to a radio receiver that detects unseen radio waves. The mind that rises from the brain bears receptors open to the vast impalpable domain of non-material laws, principles and moral concerns that govern the cosmos.

If there is any human progress it might be compared to the automobile. A modern vehicle looks very unlike those of the early 20th Century. Yet there are common basic features. They all have four tires on the road and they transport people. The appearance of the automobile body is different, but the function is the same.

So, to ask the question again: Has human society made progress? In science and technology the answer is unquestionably yes. In the area of moral choice, while we are guided by certain timeless concerns, the record is spotty at best. As you have rightly suggested, our moral choices of today differ in context but not in essence. Will there ever be progress on this front? I doubt we will ever know.

3

Spirituality

At almost every level and in almost all Christian churches, the idea of spirituality is a given. But what does it mean? And should it be part of daily life? Perhaps spirituality isn't that simple a matter.

Mick: Spirituality is the opium of those who cannot fully face the challenges of a world in which humanity has come of age. Just as some seek refuge in drink and drugs, so also do some religious people shelter from reality in spiritual practices.

Now, Rick, you may shrink from this judgment because it is too harsh, too over-the-top. Be that as it may, I intend to argue it to the limit.

So let me kick off by suggesting first that the spiritual cannot be described except in subjective terms. I can only be told about it. And what is absolutely subjective cannot be verified by an observer.

I conclude that a spiritual experience is a mental state. Practices which produce such states are pursued by some because they prove rewarding in some way. I don't deny that. But in the final resort that is all that so-called spirituality is. No more, no less.

Rick: Definitions of spirituality are numerous, variable and personal. There are common elements. Before specifically addressing your introductory comments I want to digress to provide a framework for my understanding of spirituality based on my theories of consciousness.

For billions of years following the "big bang" the cosmos expanded and evolved, essentially unobserved. Then suddenly (figuratively speaking) all changed with the rise of conscious *Homo sapiens*. A fork in the evolutionary path was reached. The cosmos now came under scrutiny by the rational human mind. Data gathered from past experience could be marshaled to control the present and help predict the future thereby lending a desirable measure of stability to life. The principle of cause and effect was recognized.

Why had all this happened and who or what was the agent, the ultimate cause of the effect? The human mind, by its very nature, divided into a rational material compartment and, for lack of a better term, a spiritual/ aesthetic or non-material one. It is the conscious individual operating in the spiritual/aesthetic mode contemplating the ultimate cause or God or first cause, whatever term you wish to use, that constitutes the basic framework of religion and spirituality however it is defined.

Many adornments can be hung on the frame such as solitude and retreat, incense, yoga, meditation, prayer or what ever you wish. But when stripped bare, the fundamental framework should appear, namely an individual standing in conscious relation to the ultimate cause.

I return to your comments. In the course of my practice I gave a lot of opium drugs to my patients who were in pain. It was the right thing to do. If spiritual practices provide respite from the material world, why shouldn't they be used? From time to time, most of us need temporary shelter from reality. A glass or two of wine may even do the trick.

All these spiritual thoughts are, of course, a subjective mental state. The very fact we are discussing this matter belies our belief that subjective experience is real and meaningful. It is just more difficult to measure than material experiences.

Mick: I'd like first to identify points of agreement. You agree that a "spiritual" event is by definition subjective. It cannot be shared or confirmed, but only reported. You also agree that a "spiritual practice" which enhances human experience is legitimate. That is, it doesn't have to be specifically Christian to, in your words, stand in "conscious relation to the ultimate cause".

So far, so good.

What I find hard to understand is that there are two fundamental dimensions. There is the universe *and* there is an ultimate cause. You think that we humans likewise comprise two compartments. One is material and another is spiritual/aesthetic.

Can you explain how you have reached those conclusions?

Rick: I have previously suggested that the very nature of the conscious human mind leads not only to the recognition and evaluation of material reality, but also raises questions about what possibly lies behind and beyond the concrete world. This is simply cause and effect logic inherent in cognition. I am neither affirming nor denying an other-world reality. I am only suggesting how I understand the function of the mind.

My conclusions about the spiritual/esthetic compartment are based in part on the following evidence:

1. Prehistoric and archeological evidence of human artistic and religious behavior;
2. Manifestations of artistic and spiritual/esthetic behavior in modern man
3. My personal spiritual/esthetic experience;
4. Scientific evidence of faith inclinations encoded in the human genome.

I suppose the hard question is, if a person does not experience or practice "spirituality", can that person still be considered a person of faith?

Mick: Drug addicts may be free of some pain, but the price is high. Part is loss of contact with life itself. Similarly, spirituality is used to "provide respite" (to quote you) from life in the round. I maintain that the price is loss of integration.

My world is a unity. It may be viewed from many angles. The spiritual/aesthetic is only one. As it happens, it's not particularly important in my life. I don't pray, for example.

Let me illustrate: Some doctors are beginning to understand the unity of the human organism. When they ask, "What are the defining characteristics of healthy living systems?" the answer comes back, "Before all else, unity."

So, by all means talk about and practice prayer, meditation and the like. But there is no need for the "spiritual". We divide the whole only to help our understanding. The resulting parts do not exist. We should not reify them.

Rick: Cloth is made of threads. Tissues are made of cells. The whole is best understood by analyzing the constituents. Were I to advise my patients on how to best lead a happy and fruitful life I would advise "balance." To balance all the elements, the material, the spiritual/aesthetic or whatever, is often difficult requiring maturity and experience. If one concentrates on one particular "compartment" over others, "imbalance", or as you might say, "disunity", is created.

Addressing the word "spirituality" has, I fear, caused us to talk around each other. I suspect "spirituality" is really a cipher for the debate concerning the existence of an immaterial reality. In this regard I would ask where does Pi reside? It must come before the drawn circle. Where do the principles governing the cosmos lie? Do they exist beyond their concrete manifestations? Where does "Radical Faith" exist, somewhere in mid-air? I guess I haven't progressed in my thinking beyond Aristotle.

I return again to the idea of personal choice. Given all the arguments that can and have been mustered for or against the concept of reality beyond the material, I see no way to settle the dispute. Considering the millions of years of human kind's evolution, the miniscule fragment I have thus far enjoyed can mean little except to me, my friends and my family. If I haven't already done it, I had better get about making personal choices in order to make sense out of the small spot I occupy in the universe.

Mick: I agree. There is no obvious way of settling the dispute. I suppose conceiving a reality beyond the material is one way of making sense of life. But it doesn't work for me.

Perhaps a way ahead might be to recognize an error of language. Certain words describe groupings or classes. A particular chair is an instance of the class "chairs". A particular circle is one of the class "circles". Circles are instances of a larger class "abstractions" and so on.

Similarly, I think "spiritual" is not a class "beyond the material" but a class "behaviors which assist us to achieve personal integration". If you can abandon what seems to me to be a category mistake, I might withdraw my charge of spirituality being a psychological opiate. Perhaps common ground might then be found.

Rick: You have introduced an interesting and creative method to analyze our discussion. I think it is appropriate that we have finally arrived at a matter of linguistics, "taxonomy of thought", as it were. In the domain of biology, class implies an ordering of categories based on features that point to a common ancestry or lineage. If this analogy is apt in our discussion, we might start by dividing reality into two kingdoms, the material and the non-material. Proceeding downward we pass through phylum, class and so forth. We can skip phylum and go directly to "class" for our purposes.

What are the features of "spirituality" that place it in the appropriate kingdom? From my perspective they are decidedly non-material. You have argued that spirituality should be in the material kingdom of the class "behaviors which assist us to achieve personal integration." Whereas spirituality may affect something on the material side, it has no material characteristics. There is no question but that spiritual exercises can result in physical changes in people. Spirituality, nonetheless, fits best in the non-material kingdom.

I share some of your suspicion of "spirituality." Its manifold expressions can range all the way from distasteful exhibitionism to secret prayer. As I previously asserted, definitions are numerous and varied. For me, I repeat, the core is a conscious person contemplating the ultimate cause. I am sure many will disagree and that is the problem. A firm definition cannot be reached and thus our taxonomy is fraught with potential error.

Language with its inherent weaknesses can be the source of disagreement and misunderstanding. As I look around my office I recognize all my apparatus, books and furniture without uttering or thinking a single word. Then my wife enters and asks to use the computer or have a piece of paper and an envelope. Suddenly everything I see has a label and I speak words. Propositional language is one of the wonders of human consciousness but it is still evolving. We continue to struggle with words in an effort to better understand our world be it material or non-material.

Mick: I had hoped to avoid our contretemps. But there it is! I remain unconvinced about spirituality as a "non-material kingdom".

As it happens, I *do* accept the non-material in a way which I suppose I could call "spiritual". But I prefer not to because of the connotations the word carries—of an alternative reality to the material universe. Perhaps my exposure in Africa to a spirit-infested world has tipped the balance.

The way in which you describe perceiving your office is something like what I mean.

To take one instance: most of us would attribute the word "immaterial" to the concept of "mind". So do I. But what I mean is that "mind" is the way you and I describe what its like being "inside" the fantastic electro-chemical system we call the "brain" (or, more correctly, the body—since we are each a total, integrated system). When we're "outside" ourselves we use a wholly different terminology for a wholly different experience of the same entity.

The same can be said, for example, about a nation. It consists entirely of physical entities. But those entities can be perceived in many non-material ways. A nation has buildings and architecture, traditions and ceremonies. Its laws are much more than words printed on paper.

In the case of both brain and nation, the whole is greater than the sum of its parts.

I think that unless the Church finds ways of relating to the world without so-called "spirituality" it will continue to shrink and die.

4

Reality

The true nature of **reality** is perhaps the greatest puzzle there is. We all live our lives out on the basis on the conclusions we come to about this puzzle. Here Rick and Mick debate whether reality includes the non-material.

Rick: From our previous dialog it is apparent we have widely divergent views of reality. I hope I have interpreted your position correctly, namely, that you believe only in material reality.

In contrast, I assert realities beyond the material domain including the idea of God or a first cause.

It is not my intention to dissuade you from your beliefs, but rather to try to understand how one comes to embrace either position. This is important, I think if either side is to gain support and adherents. I have read surveys that indicate a majority of scientists—prototypes of materialism—support your position. I would point out that many eminent scientists also believe in a non-material reality.

It is ironic that you, based in a religious profession, are in the material camp whereas I, whose professional life was grounded in science, find myself in a dual position.

I respect the importance of materiality but at the same time find critical importance for living in believing in non-material things.

How did we come to such different views of life?

Mick: For much of my life I would have agreed with you. That is, I would have supported the proposition that the world we each experience is not all there is. I would have been hard-pressed to demonstrate that reality extends beyond the material. But I was nevertheless convinced that God is, as it were, the "ground of our being". I thought I would one day experience in full what I now experience in part.

I have never abandoned the possibility.

But it now seems to me that it is a possibility without conclusive evidence. Indeed I am unable to point to any convincing evidence at all. Many people tell me of a non-material reality. None is able to show it to me in any shape or form.

My mention of "evidence" is revealing, I suppose. Be that as it may, it seems to me now that there is no point in living as though there are *any* conclusive answers at all. I am convinced about some truths—but only as long as the evidence for those truths is sufficient. In my book, every truth is provisional.

I have often been pitied by those who "believe" in the non-material. It's true that I lose the sure and certain comfort they claim for themselves. But I gain much, much more.

Rick: "Evidence." That is a key word in this discussion. It brings to mind the words of St Thomas:"Unless I see in his hands the print of the nails, and place my finger in the mark of the nails and place my hand in his side, I will not believe" (John 20.25). Thomas was acting like a modern scientist. He set forth specific criteria to falsify the hypothesis that Jesus Christ was living having been resurrected from the dead.

Materialists say there is no "evidence" of a non-material reality. It follows to ask, what are the criteria or standards to be met for such evidence? How is the hypothesis, "There is no non-material reality," to be tested?

It is commonly argued that the presence of suffering and evil in the world is evidence of the absence of God. Since there is a mix of both bad (suffering and evil) and good (all sorts of things such as nobility, charity, love, hope, etc.) it is problematic to affirm the hypothesis there is no God or non-material reality.

Here is my question, Mick: What are your standards and criteria for "evidence" of the sort we are discussing?

Mick: I can't respond to the hypothesis, "There is no non-material reality".

First, it is impossible to produce conclusive evidence to support a negative. The assertion that "There are no six-footed mongooses" can't be investigated except by examining each and every mongoose. And even then, the last one might be missed down some hole or other.

Second, our debate is about the positive assertion, "There is a non-material reality". It is up to the person asserting this to supply evidence for its truth.

You ask what sort of evidence I need. This is a tall order for a few lines, so let me try some broad suggestions:

1. I want to experience non-material reality. To be convincing it should be of the same strength and quality as my experience of the keyboard I'm presently typing on. Ultimately, I suppose, this boils down to the kind of evidence which supports the existence of a material reality. As philosophers have noted for a long time, it is possible to reasonably dispute even this sort of reality.
2. Alternatively, I might be convinced if it were of the type of experience called "falling in love". That is, the vast majority of the human race attests to it. Only those who have never fallen in love might dispute it. But this is a wobbly sort of evidence if only because the vast majority just might be wrong.

Rick: Invoking a materialist argument to prove or disprove the existence of God or non-material reality is not appropriate. There is no experiment I can contrive that would be able to test the hypothesis. Nor can I envision any material manifestation that would convince a materialist even though it bore the label, "made by God in heaven."

Requiring materialist evidence serves only to dismiss the question.

The second line of evidence you cite is more congenial to the discussion. A consensus of shared subjective experience can be forceful support (for some) for a non-material reality. Such a consensus exists but it is not unanimous. It leaves the issue still undecided. It is an impossible argument.

What I want to try to understand is how each individual person adopts either side of the issue. It is my observation there are "tipping points" when either external events or other persons create conditions that tip the balance to either side.

I have only a few close friends. Whereas they all once identified with the church, most if not all no longer do. From what they have shared with me it seems it was the arrogance and hypocritical behavior of representatives and some members of the church that turned them away.

As for me I continue to have my doubts from time to time. But on balance I am still in the fold of believers. My balance has been tipped not only by family traditions but moreover by the wondrous group of people who have been my "spiritual" mentors. Examples of people seem more influential than doctrinal details.

I return to my introductory question: How did we come to such different views of life?

Mick: I don't know. Perhaps upbringing ("family tradition") is the clincher. Or perhaps unhelpful behavior of Christians tips the balance for some. Maybe social pressures push some people into one or other position.

I have been influenced by non-Christian family and friends. I also recognize and honor fellow Christians who have very different conclusions about reality and yet have been kind, generous and accepting towards me.

I have tried over the years to stay with the hypothesis that there is a non-material reality. I find that neither reason nor experience allow me to do that any longer. In other words, I hope I have, by and large, thought my way to my present position. However, I will change that position if persuaded.

Rick: It is clear, Mick, we are both still on our separate journeys toward truth. We have quite different ideas of what lies beyond the door of death; and what, who or if anything has given form to the world and the cosmos. I think we have *both* used reason in our respective searches. Can reason alone clarify all the ambiguities and mysteries? I am not sure but I don't think so.

It is suggested that the church is in trouble because it adheres to creeds that make no material sense as for instance the resurrection of Jesus Christ (as well as others). Waning identification with the church, particularly in Europe, is cited as evidence for this view. It suggests that reality is a zero sum game. That is to say, as material reality is progressively defined the church and religion in general will fade away.

As I have stated previously, I contend the human mind has two co-equal compartments, the material and the spiritual/aesthetic. Each has its own rules, vocabulary and imagery. Each compartment informs the other but they co-exist, side by side. I know this dualism causes you to bridle but that is the way I can best explain my life experience. As long as humans exist they will always require nourishment of the spiritual/aesthetic compartment no matter how thoroughly the material world is defined.

Mick: I'm personally more than content that you approach reality the way you do. As you mentioned above, I'm "based in a religious profession". So you can appreciate that most people around me have concluded much as you do. I find that I can get on with them perfectly well because I keep my convictions to myself most of the time. For example, I participate as best I can in acts of worship which assume a non-material reality.

The clincher in daily life is that the practical requirements of love rise above petty squabbling about the map of a country to which nobody has ever been.

But I nevertheless do experience a sense of isolation. Some have dubbed it living in exile—an image with which I have considerable sympathy. I regard myself as a Christian. But given half the chance, many Christians would seek to drive me out because of my position. So you will appreciate why I take considerable care to avoid the deadly sting of the inquisition.

However, as I have already suggested, I gain much from my way of life. There is a sense of integration. The entire body of human knowledge fits together. There will always be mystery, always the unexplained. But I'm convinced that it all hangs together in a glorious system.

I am challenged to be autonomous. There is no need for parental guidance from heaven. I can, if I so choose, experience true adulthood. Add to that a certain frisson of risk. My life has no certainties, no complete security. What I do, I do knowing that my choice may turn out wrong. What I know, I know only for now, not for ever.

The upshot is that a person who lives in this world lives a life of discovery and growth. Because nothing is finally settled, all is movement. I think I may have turned my back for ever on the idea that somewhere over the rainbow is a heavenly Land of Oz where all is perfect, all is peace.

5

Prayer

I f any activity is universally prescribed by Christian churches it is **prayer**. Many sermons are preached about it. A growing practice of spiritual guidance aims to assist people in prayer. But thinking about the subject turns up some intractable difficulties as well as valuable opportunities.

Mick: Paul Walker describes how he once thought of prayer as "the oxygen of faith". It was touted to him as "a two-way conversation with the Almighty, a massive privilege". The trouble was, he writes, "I could never really manage it myself".

My experience over 40 years of being a Christian has been similar. I have spent many, many hours dutifully praying to God and Jesus. But all the while I wondered why I heard only my own voice. If God and Jesus did speak to me in response, why couldn't I hear them?

Similarly, a mentor once advised me to practice what he called an "arrow prayer". "When you see a tramp or alcoholic on the street, or meet someone who looks ill or troubled, just aim a quick thought—like an arrow—to God," he said. I found that this helped me. But it appeared to have zero effect on the people prayed for.

Perhaps, Rick, you can advise me. I'm not so cocksure as to suppose that many before me have not had similar experiences.

Rick: The following remarks are predicated on my belief in a non-material reality and God.

I like the simple definition of prayer found in Webster's dictionary: "To address God with adoration, confession, supplication or thanksgiving." To address God is an act of faith that there is a God, that he (or she: I'd prefer not to get into that tortuous argument of gender so I will continue in the masculine) is receptive to us and is disposed to respond to our prayers.

Furthermore, prayer is essentially a *conscious act* wherein we are aware of what we are saying to God. Is it possible our unconscious minds pray? I don't know how we can apprehend this possibility so it must remain moot. Quite likely our subconscious mind continually processes thoughts and feeds them upward into consciousness; but it is the conscious state that is the final arbiter of the content. In the conscious state we weigh choices deliberately. Consciousness enables free will or choice. Consciousness is required for moral decisions.

Prayer is a conscious recognition of the primacy of God in our lives. It defines a relationship and solidarity similar to children and parents maintaining their affection for one another. The most important element is our striving to have a relationship with God. Having established this relationship it is hard for me to imagine how considerations of quantity or quality of prayer have any meaning. God can't be bribed. He will not suspend the natural law He created simply to relieve our suffering. If we stand in awe of the creator and have trust in him we must view everything as gift, even the bad.

I am reminded of the physician who comes into the hospital room of a severely ill patient. The air is filled with alarm and dread. The patient and onlookers are in anguish. The physician calms the air and stills the alarm with coolness, authority and compassion. Perhaps the final outcome is not affected by his words or actions but the anxiety and mental pain have been calmed. In our prayers we ought to seek the coolness and grace of God. We may wish for different outcomes of our dilemmas; that may or may not be realized but we should always ask for courage to withstand all of life's challenges. The most important petition is for the maintenance of our faith in God.

How does God intervene in the world? Does he use magic tricks? I don't think so. There is obviously much mystery in the manner in which God could intercede in our affairs. God could use us to effect the petitions of our prayers. In this context it is appropriate to break down prayer into private and public.

In our private prayers, God can help us clarify our thoughts to find solutions achievable with our own resources. He can serve as counselor infusing us with knowledge and insights yielding positive conscious action.

In public prayer a broad spectrum of people are exposed to petitions and may be galvanized to respond to them. We, the people, are the major reservoir of agents for action on prayer. I think God knows our thoughts and desires so that any verbalization of prayer must be for the attention of the hearers. When we petition out loud we are hoping others will hear and be energized to action.

Mick: Your exposition raises many queries. One is to ask what makes you think that God is interested in our adoration, confession, supplication and thanksgiving?

I for one have long since ceased relating to anyone either as parent or as the sort of physician you describe. Yes, life is full of blessings and joys. But it's also crammed with real terrors which no physician, divine or otherwise, can mitigate.

Anyway, what mature, balanced person would either ask or require that others relate to him or her in the manner you describe? In my book such a person would be pathologically egotistical.

I grant that public prayer is another kettle of fish. Yes, it energizes us to action. But if that's its function, if it works as a corporate sign and covenant, why is so much of it framed in such self-demeaning, sycophantic terms?

Rick: I agree that prayers can be framed in self-demeaning and sycophantic terms. I also agree that there are such things as pathologic egotists. These realities are consistent with the flawed nature of mankind that could well use some guidance and correction.

I have encountered many persons whom I considered mature and balanced who sought counsel and strength in times of adversity. As a "pathologic egotist" I felt constrained by empathy to be of assistance.

Despite all the pitfalls and problems with pryer that you cite, I do not see how any of them disqualify it as a valuable and effective instrument for many people.

I have great respect for those who face all problems solely with their own resources. Such total command of life I have not yet achieved nor do I think total self-reliance would make my life better. Self-sufficiency can deprive one of rewarding interpersonal relationships. Interdependence with individuals and communities is not a bad thing. In fact, I see it as a necessary feature of civil society.

Is God interested in our adoration, confession, supplication and thanksgiving? Answers to this question hinge on one's conception of God. If he does not exist, the question is irrelevant. If he is indifferent to creation, the question is moot. The answer is yes if you believe God not only exists but has, as well, a personal dimension.

I do not consider prayer as placation of God but, rather, as a natural human impulse to make contact with the holy and to consciously create a relationship with transcendent power.

Mick: Fair enough. I'd like you now to try the following on for size. It's another way of approaching prayer which may fit you—or anyway, may find a place in your wardrobe.

Prayer for me consists of two streams. These streams are unusual in that they mix and separate, each constantly enriching the other yet retaining its own character.

The first stream is my prayer as an individual. Prayer flows through my whole being. There is no spiritual tributary and the flow never ceases. I am constantly immersed in life. As I live I pray and I pray while I live. Currents of prayer fertilize my life. They help me grow into specific life-creating activities in my tiny part of the world. At the same time, I note and stay aware of aspects of life in stretches of the stream beyond my reach.

The second stream is public prayer. I pray as an individual during public prayer. But I also take part in a corporate affirmation of life. I join with like-minded people in a mighty river of celebration. These waters potentially nurture everyone, without exception. They include sorrow for personal and corporate failings, best expressed publicly because of their intertwined nature. The place of a community in the greater river is celebrated and mutual concerns expressed. But it is in the main a celebration in many differing forms of the creation in all its glory.

Anyone can pray like this, though as a Christian I pray personally and corporately with Jesus of Nazareth in the forefront of my consciousness.

Rick: One of the most important faculties of the human mind is propositional speech. We communicate with each other with language to share ideas and feelings. We can literally open our minds to our fellow beings. This stands in bold contrast to other species who merely signal each other in rudimentary matters of survival.

Our communications, or better, our conversations imply the presence of an interlocutor, one with whom we are trying to share our ideas and feelings. Talking with self is thinking, not conversation. There must be someone outside of self with whom to speak.

In prayer the interlocutor is God. We do not pray to our fellow humans. We might admonish them but we do not pray to them.

When we affirm life and celebrate life-creating activities we are not praying. We are taking conscious note, marking them as positive and fulfilling events or qualities. Celebration alone has no interlocutor. There is a vast difference between thinking about something and entering into a conversation about it. Prayer is a conversation with someone or some power beyond the human.

Our discussion of prayer has once again highlighted our different views of reality. If there is no God or higher being then, I submit, there can be no prayer; instead, there are only discussions, speculations, commiserations, etc. about the nature of the human experience. For some this is sufficient. For countless others prayer is a vital life-sustaining act that gives purpose and meaning to their lives.

How each person arrives at either side of the divide is a complex matter as we have already discussed. What I consider most important is for each individual to be aware of the choices involved and to take the path that will lead to the best outcome in this short lifetime.

Mick: Yes, our discussion of prayer illustrates beautifully the gulf between traditional Christianity and Christianity in exile. There seems no way of bridging the chasm.

The old picture portrays a world foreign to me. I must take it out of the frame and store it with due reverence. Into the frame goes the world I know.

The new picture is spoilt if I brush in God as a person. So what I paint is God in-between everything—between the insubstantial strings of energy which make up atomic particles, between the weakest whiffs of interstellar gas in the vast reaches of space/time, between the very neurons of our brains.

This is not a person, but personality itself—indescribably intimate, yet encompassing all. I trust that this in-between God knows and intimately shares the world in my picture frame.

The picture I create can't converse with me. But it does in a strange way communicate with me as I look at it.

So what is important is that I constantly affirm the life which animates the canvass—my life, the life of others, the life of the universe. I conflict with elements which seek to paint life out of the image. On my part there is a constant refocusing, a constant envisioning, and a constant readjustment of the brush strokes. This process I call prayer.

6

Religion

Religion in its many forms remains for the vast majority of people worldwide a primary factor in their lives. Religions are many and varied. Some are happy to exist side-by-side with differing religions. Other religions show limited tolerance of rivals. In the modern age, secularism displays a singular lack of interest in religion as a necessary social force.

Rick: For the moment, let us put aside our argument about materialism versus non-materialism and consider *religion* in its own right irrespective of its genesis. Religion has been around a long time, suggesting to me it is an important feature of the human psyche.

We are both aware of the terrible things done in the name of religion. Currently the Middle East fulminates due in large part to religious issues. The crusades, the inquisition, anti-Semitism and other religiously motivated cataclysms stand as indictments of various organized religious entities.

My question to you, Mick, is: Do you think organized religion is a positive or negative influence in human society?

Mick: Let me be plain at the outset that if I were never again to attend a church service I would experience little or no regret. Religion is to me like a symphony to a tone-deaf person.

And so to your question. I think that religion is like the curate's egg. Some may know of the famous cartoon in the magazine *Punch* in 1895. It shows an obsequious young clergyman at one end of a long table, his bishop at the other. The bishop remarks, "I'm afraid you've got a bad egg, Mr. Jones." Replies the curate, "Oh no, my Lord, I assure you! Parts of it are excellent!"

And so with religion. Those aspects which enhance self-worth I find pleasing. So also the parts which provide accepting, supportive fellowship. But those which promote bigotry, intolerance and ideology I regard as profoundly damaging to humanity.

Rick: Before proceeding further I think it advisable to define *religion*. I offer the following: In its simplest reduction it is a conscious person standing in relation to what they regard as holy, sacred or divine. When a number of individuals of similar beliefs join together and develop some kind of unifying doctrine it is called organized religion. Prime examples include Christianity, Judaism and Islam. All religions are predicated on a non-material reality, a discussion we will not enter at this point.

Bigotry, intolerance and ideology are not confined to religion. I would even say they might be found less frequently in religion than in secular institutions. It is a mindless task trying to apportion blame. Bigotry, intolerance and ideology are bad no matter where they emanate. When a religion fails to reflect values of goodness and humanity, the failure is magnified and considered hypocritical. Similar failures by secular institutions may incur only a sigh and shake of the head as nothing more is expected. On reviewing my experience with religion (in this case being a lifelong Lutheran) the scale tips heavily to the good side. If I could not regularly attend church services I am sure I would be disoriented in the world. I have seen my church pour out vast amounts of charity to needy persons; I have seen consolation given to the grieving; I have witnessed strength rendered in adversity. I will not go on to give more examples as you know whereof I speak.

Here is my next question: What if all religions were suddenly to disappear leaving only the secular world. What would the world look like and what would fill the void vacated by religion? Would there be a different quality to charity, consolation and strength?

Mick: I prefer Lloyd Geering's description of religion (from the Latin *religio*, meaning an attitude of devotion):

A conscientious concern for what really matters . . . not a concrete noun naming a thing but an abstract noun referring to a state of being . . .

I know very few people who are not religious in this way. But I suspect that what we're discussing here is the institutional expression of religion by Christians in particular.

Unlike you I have spent many years completely outside the Church. I found no difference between religious people and secular people. Some of the former—especially Christians and Muslims—tended to recite doctrines which they claimed were absolutely true for everyone without exception. This tended to get in the way of solving difficult mutual problems.

You're correct that bigotry, intolerance and ideology are present everywhere. However, a critical difference between Christianity and the secular world is that the former claims to be motivated by a deep love for the world as exemplified by a certain Jesus of Nazareth.

If so, I say they have peculiar ways of showing it. Jesus accepted everyone, refused the rule of religion, and chose death rather than give up his friends. The Church accepts others only on its own terms, exerts ruthless power over its members, and will sacrifice the individual for its own safety.

But, thank goodness, Christianity is not essentially a religion but a way of life.

Rick: You did not respond directly to my question as to what the world would look like if all religions were to suddenly disappear. However, I infer from your remarks that you probably think, if the moral climate were not better, at least it would be less hypocritical. Did I understand you correctly?

I will not quibble about our definitions of religion. I am sure there are many that would fit the scope of this discussion. I agree, the main focus of this debate concerns, ". . . the institutional expression of religion by Christians in particular." There are issues you raise concerning the Church's demeanor that are provocative and not very complimentary. Not being a theologian I must defer to your superior knowledge of scripture and doctrine to clarify some points for me.

First, you seem uncomfortable with any form of authority and absolutism. Christ said: "I am the way and the truth and the life; no one comes to the Father but by me." (John 14:6) This has the ring of absolutism and authoritarianism to me. Or, do you reject the historical authenticity of the statement?

As for Christ's acceptance of *everyone* he was quite un-accepting of the money changers and a few Pharisees not to mention others. He was quite un-hypocritical in his enmity and I think correctly so. Do you think the blanket acceptance of *everyone* irrespective of their behavior is necessary to be a Christian or is this Polyannaish?

You assert the Church is exclusionary, exerts ruthless power and sacrifices individuals for its own safety. In citing these actions, are you constructing an absolutist code of proper behavior? Or are these simply passing offenses that have meaning only in context of which side of the issue one finds himself? Does the Church have the right of *survival* as we discussed some time ago?

I need your help in clarifying these issues.

Mick: I'm not saying that Christians as a group are hypocritical. But I am pointing out that love of others is the Church's self-proclaimed fundamental priority. Actions which contradict that must be questioned. Institutional Christianity can't have its cake and eat it, though it tries to do just that.

For more than a century now a majority of scholars has agreed that your quotation from John's Gospel are the words of its author, not of Jesus—though the news hasn't been given much space in the pews. In contrast, the money-changers incident, minus some likely accretions, is probably historical. But I don't know for sure what Jesus meant by this action.

Whatever its meaning, I have little doubt that acceptance of everyone was the overall stand Jesus took. The historical evidence for this I regard as overwhelming.

The Church has distorted this unconditional acceptance. Baptism, for example, was at first a ritual sign that a person had boarded the Christian ship. Today it is a ticket allowing a person on board. That is, the Church has become a club which restricts entrance to membership and access to its sacraments. This is not true to Jesus.

It's likely that organized religion will remain a valid and viable way for many Christians to express their "conscientious concern for what really matters". But I doubt that it is a "feature of the human psyche", as you put it. That would make it *sine qua non* to every human. It clearly isn't that. Many millions have a deep commitment to life and the love of others without it. In short, religion is optional. It is useful to some, but not essential to all.

So the essence of being Christian is not to be religious but to live a certain type of life. This way of life looks to Jesus as one—for some *the* one—upon whose pioneering lifestyle a person's being can be fashioned. Some Christians seek to sanitize this way of life through the Church as institution. Control of ritual, doctrine and ethics expressed in absolutist terms is essential to achieve this. The final sanction is to exclude those who don't toe the line. They become expendable outcasts.

When this happens, as it so frequently does, religion becomes evil. When it becomes evil it has no more right to survive than any other evil institution.

Rick: As a physician I am particularly aware of the importance of history. It is critical in formulating a diagnosis (reality). As an expert witness in many medico-legal cases I have experienced how uncertain and malleable the truth can be. As time recedes from the present, the problem of inaccuracy of the facts increases. Thus, any body of information must be tested on the basis of accepted sources unless and until these sources are impeached by unassailable and demonstrable facts.

You assert that a majority of scholars say the words written in the gospel of John are not those of Jesus. I think to revise the history of 2000 years ago is at best a stretch. History is made up not only of putative fact but is, as well, laced with the bias of its author. The realities of historiography leave us with more speculation than certainty. To say the words reported in John are false or inaccurate is to engage in a fruitless polemic. If the divinity of Christ is not accepted there are no aspects of the historical record supporting his transcendence that will be accepted by detractors. Those who ascribe to Christ's divinity will of course select facts that support their belief. It is a never ending process.

So who is Christ? Is He simply an historic person? Who has the canon of Christology? The Church relies on the account of Holy Scripture. You have said he accepted everyone. I disagree. Furthermore I think that unqualified acceptance of everyone is not necessarily a criterion of ultimate goodness. *Acceptance* probably means many things to many people Do you accept Adolph Hitler or Joseph Stalin?

If suppression of the individual is a test for evil, then I submit all of secular society is culpable and, therefore, has no right to survive. In this context, including the sometimes errant Church in the company of Nazi Tyranny, Stalinism and the Holocaust is intemperate and serves only to trivialize evil.

Finally, I am puzzled how one can be considered an "outcast" from an organization he has not joined. The Church is founded on the metaphysical premise of transcendent non-materialism. If this is not accepted it is illogical to claim membership. Were I such an outcast I might consider joining with friends of like-mind to create a Jesus club and rid myself of the problem.

7

Authority

The Church claims **authority** to preach absolute truths to all mankind. These are truths which, we are told, affect every human being at an absolutely fundamental level.

Mick: Years ago I worked in the South African mining industry. It faces peculiar difficulties, particularly in gold mines which go down some 3 000 meters.

Safety concerns are understandably paramount in that dangerous environment, so the chief executive is accountable in law for everything that happens on the mine. He can be jailed if a supervisor at the rock face takes a safety shortcut and someone is hurt or killed. But the supervisor can't easily be prosecuted because he has no authority to specify what's safe and what isn't.

In business, managers are authorized by a board or similar body. They in turn derive authority from shareholders who get their authority from the laws of the land, passed by politicians. The latter are authorized by the voters to pass laws. In the case of democracies, therefore, voters are the ultimate source of authority.

Authority, then, is on one hand the right to give commands, and on the other the acceptance of possible penalties for errors and omissions. Authority without accountability is tyranny. Accountability without authority is oppression.

As I understand it, Church leaders give God as the ultimate source of their authority. I find this claim unconvincing.

Rick: Death and taxes, we are told, are the only certain things in life. I would revise the old aphorism to include *authority.* To avoid chaos, there is a natural drive for individuals and societies to coalesce around figures or institutions having authority.

From early morning to late in the day and even when we sleep we are all subject to authority. There is authority in the family circle, at our work places, when we drive on the highways and when we identify with a church.

As you suggest, authority derives from some hierarchical source and has varying degrees of gravity and consequence. It is one thing to exercise authority as a parent and another to act as a police officer.

We submit to authority either voluntarily or by coercion. In a free society I can quit my job if I don't like the authority. I can divorce my wife. Or, I can leave my church if I am uncomfortable with its authority. When I bomb a government building I will be coerced to submit if I am caught.

Sources of authority can be logically traced to the particular nature of the institution or the role of the individual exercising authority. Parental authority is based on cultural norms. Business authority is derived from business models and applicable business law. Since the Church is founded on belief in God, it should not be surprising it claims authority from that source.

Mick: I think we agree broadly on the *nature* of authority. If I were to wonder about an aspect of your admirable summary it would be with regard to the reciprocal nature of human authority.

As we have noted, accountability operates upwards in a hierarchy, usually in a complex web reinforced by a formal structure of some sort. The strength of democracy is that accountability is returned to the bottom of the pile. Subjects can dismiss their rulers and appoint others. In other words, accountability should include the possibility of sanctions. We in the West speak of authority without accountability in terms such as dictatorship, autocracy and despotism.

As I understand you, members of the Church do not operate under this sort of authority. Their authority is derived from God, and they therefore answer to God. God, by definition, cannot be called to account.

I am stumped by this line of thought. It is as though I'm operating blind. That is, I can't check out the God side of the equation. I find no way of challenging the statement "I have God's authority" except by dismissing the "God" part of it.

Rick: To those who are frank materialists or atheists, the following remarks will sound banal. For those who believe in God I hope I will make sense. I happen to live in both the materialist and non-materialist worlds, adapting both to my particular situations.

As God is the creator of all reality it is absurd to think He can be accountable for anything. He is the autocrat of the universe, the benign despot of the world. As one descends from the source of all authority into the sphere of humanity, authority is less authentic. Those who assert authority from God can be held accountable and challenged for their interpretations of God's will. One of my icons, Martin Luther, did just that.

I believe that moral authority that is consistent and enduring is founded on a source beyond the physical contingencies of life. If it is not, it will always ebb and flow at the whim of any earthly despot or societal change.

Although Christ lived two thousand years ago amidst vastly different social circumstances, His concerns, as I interpret them, resonate to this day. They are, as I asserted in our debate on *Progress*, concerns for:

1. human life;
2. individual dignity;
3. personal identity and integrity;
4. one's neighbor and society;
5. the significance of human existence.

These are unchangeable concerns, bearing authority, emanating from a source beyond the physical. They are dynamic principles that can be applied to any contingency or circumstance.

Mick: Don't get me wrong. Anyone can assert beliefs. But I'm assuming that all such assertions are best tested. So let me try to test yours. Here's a case:

> Christian A asserts that x is the truth from God about the significance of human existence.

Christian B asserts that y is God's truth about human existence and that A is therefore incorrect.

I am someone who believes in God. I acknowledge the existence of an authority beyond the material who gives us principles to apply to any contingency or circumstance. I note that the assertions of Christians A and B contradict each other. What criteria do I apply to choose between them?

In other words, I'm asking how and on what authority I'm to know that Luther was correct and his opponents misguided.

Rick: Two thousand years ago Pontius Pilate asked, "What is truth?" We have asked the same question throughout these debates and quite likely a similar question was in the minds of the earliest *Homo sapiens.* There is a kind of arrogance to the present that compels us to think we will and must have solutions to everything in our lifetimes. The Middle East problem will be solved, poverty will be abolished, justice will ultimately be served to all who seek it; on and on it goes. Most likely we ride in a stream with no final resting place of truth. *C'est la vie ET c'est la le diable.*

In the meantime, we of fleeting existence must try to make the best possible deal with our lives. Our individual "truths" derive from those sources and authorities we trust (if they are not forced on us) be they traditions, civil laws, religions or charismatic persons.

As for the two disagreeing Christians A and B, I must know more about their assertions x and y before I can judge who has the truth. They both may be right. To use the analogy of the great mountain, each could be viewing it from different flanks but still describing the same mountain.

Despite these ambiguities, I perceive threads of universality and truth weaving through, not only the wondrous material world, but as well through the sublime reality of non-materiality. These universals are, in part, embodied in the five major concerns I previously enumerated. Knowledge of these principles is afforded each human being by virtue of a conscious mind. If we were not conscious, of what significance or use would be truth?

Mick: I acknowledge that meaning for a person depends on perspective and that contradictions may arise when attempting to fuse differing perspectives. There will therefore always be mysteries.

The question here relates to authority. I must press you on it. None of us can see from all perspectives and many answers must perforce be accepted on trust. But mistakes are easily made. I wonder why you trust your authorities. Are they open to questioning? By what means were their answers arrived at? Are their answers supported by anyone else? Are conflicting answers just as valid as theirs? These are all critical questions for me.

We can't test all who claim authority, though I think we should test as many as we can—including those who claim to derive authority from beyond the physical. For example, the Pope says that God forbids abortion except in rare, clearly defined cases. The problem for me is that God is unavailable for questioning.

Rick: You, as a sovereign conscious individual, have the right to question any one, but not God or Jesus Christ who is an extension of God. Any human below this level is, in my book, fair game. Whether or not you are successful is another question. Those you may challenge have the same right to question your truth and your motives. As a young man I questioned many authority figures and often came out second best. In retrospect I was probably basing my challenges more on opinion than on truth. Then again, I feel I was sometimes right in the light of the truth I held. There are timeless, unalterable truths and there are mere opinions.

I am struck by how, in this discussion, the words "truth" and "authority" are found in juxtaposition. They really go together. Real authority is founded on truth. Authority without truth is not authentic. As always, the rub comes in trying to find truth and to argue what is important and not trivial.

I still believe there are basic, immutable truths such as those expressed in the five concerns. More often than not, truth comes dressed in modern packaging that must be unwrapped to find the nugget. Truth in this sense is not relative, but only seen in a mirror dimly. It comes hidden and in versions.

Thus, I say challenge whom you will. Good luck with the Pope.

Mick: You have me between a rock and a hard place!

On one hand I cannot assert any final authority because I have none except my own reasoning capacity. That is, I have taken the position that in the final resort I must decide for myself what's true about life and what isn't. And when I say "true", I find I mean only "most likely".

On the other hand, I can't question the authority "emanating from a source beyond the physical" which you propose because I have found no way of accessing it.

So I'm damned if I do and damned if I don't.

Which is, I suppose, why I regard myself as an exile from traditional Christianity. That is, the Church offers me only damnation. Or, to put it another way, Jesus is for me to be found mainly outside the Church.

8

Freedom

Did Jesus intend to found the Church? Did he appoint a set of office bearers with clearly defined job descriptions and a set of official teachings?

Rick: "Individualism" is a salient feature of most free societies. It stands in contrast to "collectivism" that characterizes closed totalitarian societies. The American Constitution specifies in the Bill of Rights how the individual is to be protected. Before the rise of liberal democratic governments, dignity of the individual was espoused in Holy Scripture. There seems to be a link between human individual freedom as a general principle and its source in a transcendent power that some call God.

Societies are composed of citizens; churches are made up of worshipers. At some point, individuals must be subsumed by the collective group to become an effective instrument for what ever purpose they gather.

It has been asserted by critics of democracy that individualism is a flaw that ultimately destroys the fabric of society. If cooperation and solidarity breakdown, (as they can in an environment of unchecked individualism) chaos can result. On the other hand, the examples of Communism and Fascism show how suppression of the individual in the name of collectivism can be devastating to societies.

Organized religion has been charged by some as being totalitarian, demanding unswerving adherence to doctrine at the expense of individual freedom of conscience. Mick, my question is, do you think the concepts and rules regarding individual freedom in the context of religion are different from those applied to the domain of politics and government?

Mick: I'm anxious not to kick off this debate in a way which makes disagreement inevitable. But that is what might happen if the individual and the corporate are taken as incompatibles.

Stating the matter from another angle might help.

As I understand it, the transforming impact of love upon people ("salvation") has from the first been spoken of by Christians at the individual level. Each of us is transformed by love ("saved") as a person. Also from the first, those who are being transformed have gathered together to express joy and mutual solidarity. There has been an ongoing tussle in the fellowship between those who emphasize love as personal (individualists) and those who think of love as best expressed through the group (collectivists).

With this in mind, I think my best answer to your question is that I don't think of love as one thing in religion and another in politics and government. The transforming love of Jesus is not constrained by human constructs and boundaries. On one hand, concepts and rules are needed to structure the fellowship. On the other, the fellowship is the *outcome* of individual transformation, not its means.

Rick: When I speak of freedom in this context I refer to the agency of the individual and how this affects the dynamic between individuals and groups. You have reframed the discussion using the force of love as a definer of the individual/group relationship. We are both looking at the same thing. There are, I am sure, many angles from which to study the issue.

Individuals and groups fit together much as walls are made of bricks and living organisms are composed of cells. There is an inescapable unity. Yet, there may be tensions and imbalances. Each individual may belong to many different groups each one having different functions and rules. I would suggest that the "fellowship" may, at least in part, be defined by individual transformation; but it is also the fellowship that shapes individual transformation. There is a constant feedback between individual and group and balance is the key.

If the brick crumbles the wall is threatened. If the cell dies the life of the organism is at risk. Any group that does not take proper and sober recognition of the individual member is not healthy. Personal identity is one of the noblest manifestations of creation.

There is no such thing as absolute freedom. Authentic freedom always has conditions and restraints. Those who deny this are likely to be ineffective in their life's goals and be detrimental to groups to which they belong. At the same time, there may arise genuinely critical occasions when the individual must stand up against the group. Where does one find the wisdom to discern these moments?

Mick: I'm no more enamored of individualism than you appear to be. For me it equates with egotism. Self-interest discounts the fact that each of us survives only as part of society. At one extreme, anarchy touts individual freedom without reciprocal responsibility.

Democracy attempts reciprocity between person and group. It is a system by which individuals band together in a dictatorship of the majority to decide matters of freedom. Which is why Theodore Roosevelt is reputed to have said of democracy that "A government can be no better than the public opinion that sustains it". Nevertheless, its main strength is that free opposition is built into the system.

Some churches govern themselves democratically. In contrast, Roman Catholics (by far the majority of Christians) prefer a self-perpetuating oligarchy. Its leaders assert that hell awaits those who refuse to give allegiance to Jesus. They define the criteria for judging if that refusal exists—and also take the power to exclude those who don't meet those criteria. In other words, Roman Catholics are not free as long as they remain within the Church or unless they subvert the system.

I would say, then, that *any* system of government, Christian or secular, which does not allow free opposition, should be opposed.

Rick: Freedom is uniquely a property of an individual conscious person. It implies the capacity for making conscious informed choices. In essence it represents the perennial idea of *free will*. Choices can be made primarily in the interest of self (egotism) or in the interest of others (altruism). What is it that tilts decisions to one side or the other?

I venture to suggest we both recognize and respect what might be called a "healthy ego." Such an ego is manifested in a person who has great self-respect but who, at the same time, expresses empathy and respect for others and the community at large. It is as though there is an instinct to transcend individual barriers to become directly involved in the thoughts and feelings of the other person; it is, as it were, a coalescence of consciousness.

How one chooses or to which side one tilts in the dynamic of egotism versus altruism must to a large extent be the result of the teachings and examples of the nurturing community. It follows to ask, what kind of community is most likely to foster "healthy egos"? Is it one disposed to consider human kind as only one of many animals, distinguished only by so-called intelligence? Or is it one that considers human kind as unique and special in creation having not only intelligence but as well a soul?

Perhaps the highest expression of freedom and free will is the decision to give up freedom and surrender to an idea or person in which one has invested total confidence. Such a contradiction is commonplace and without apparent logic. Freedom itself is not a virtue. It is how it is used that gives it meaning. When one opposes a system because it "does not allow free opposition" might not that opposition represent the height of egotism?

Mick: I think we agree that balance between individual freedom and group solidarity is the essence of health. If balance is disturbed for too long either way, harm results.

If you or I sacrifice ourselves—say in war, or some other way—it is as part of a group that we do so. However, submission to the group is (or should be) always temporary. It aims to preserve the group now so that individuals will prosper through it in the future. It is a great lie that a group exists for itself and that the individual can therefore be sacrificed for it. It is a lie because behind it are always power-hungry people willing to cheat and enslave others for their own purposes.

The first task of a despot is to eliminate opposition and claim absolute obedience from the individual. So I'm uncomfortable about the idea that freedom can be equated with "surrender to an idea or person". I think the concept may derive from a traditional Christian understanding of the ideal way to relate to God. But it seems to me that one of the ways in which the Christian faith is changing substitutes for this idea one which stresses personal autonomy in the service of others.

In other words, God is less and less the parent or boss who insists we do what we're told. Instead, God is being perceived as growing people to their full potential within the constraints of creation. That growth, I maintain, requires optimum balance between group and individual.

Rick: For the most part, we share common views about individual freedom and group solidarity. There is one aspect I would like to discus a little further before we quit this topic. It has to do with *commitment* as I expressed in my statement "surrender to an idea or person." The idea of commitment is as old as the rational, conscious mind of humankind. It is as axiomatic as mathematical equations. Commitment is not unique to Christianity or to any other religion.

I believe that commitment is often the essential ingredient in success of marriage or a job. If one has the paranoia that bogeymen are always lurking in our personal relationships and civic affairs, eagerly waiting to devour our wealth and autonomy, then we will be impaired in our ability to establish lasting relationships or commitments. I agree we should maintain a realistic skepticism about the motives of persons in authority but it should not be a pervasive, all-consuming mind set. That is an unhealthy balance.

Commitment may be viewed as a spectrum ranging from never (the egotist) to always (the altruist). There are dangers to being on either extreme. There are always risks in any range of the spectrum. Perhaps I am a romantic and see that commitment and risk-taking give life a dimension and spice that make it truly human.

Mick: We have been addressing freedom in relation to the individual on one hand and the group on the other. The individual can't mature to full potential without the group. And the group which doesn't exist for that purpose must be suspect.

In other words, I'm saying that the group which facilitates the growth of all to full maturity has my commitment. Indeed, there's a sense in which the ability to be a supportive, generous part of such a group is essential to individual maturity.

So commitment for me is a given. It's a necessary part of relationships.

At the heart of the matter is the question, "To what and who do I commit myself?" Not all groups are worthy of that commitment. Nor is every person. Recognizing that some groups and some people are evil or on the way to it, is not paranoia but plain good sense.

The difficulty is to know beforehand which is worthy and which not.

And there's the rub.

9

Inclusiveness

Fierce conflicts are on the go in the Church about its membership. The Roman Catholic Church continues its centuries-old hunt for heretics. Other churches sniff out gay clergy engaged in sexual activity. Yet others chase away liberals who are not "biblical".

Mick: Some years ago I was fortunate enough to holiday in Zimbabwe. Memories of my boyhood came flooding back—the sounds and smells of the African bush, the wide open spaces, the grass and trees and a host of other familiar tones and shades almost beyond awareness.

The month was October, when daytime temperatures in the Zambesi valley can rise to 45 degrees or more. The land was parched and the roads dusty. Brown, scorched grass lay thin on the poor soil. To a casual observer it seemed that everything was in suspended animation, waiting for the rains to come.

And yet life was everywhere in abundance, particularly around the water holes and farm dams. Animals and insects can do with little food for a long while. But without water they quickly die.

All this was in stark contrast to the lush, fertile green fields of England, where I live. Here water is abundant and food plentiful—yet wild life is scarce. Insects are few. One must go to the wilds of Scotland to be properly bitten. Wild life is tolerated only within prescribed bounds.

The world outside the Church is like the Zambesi bush. It's beautiful yet dangerous. Life is prescribed by death—that is the nature of things. Yet it seethes with abundant energy, boiling and roiling with multiple life forms, constantly alert, constantly changing, always creating.

In contrast, the Church is like the neat, manicured, engineered fields of England where wild life is fenced in, carefully controlled. People are largely out of touch with the life-forces upon which they depend. Anyone who doesn't match strict entry criteria is turned away at its borders. Anything too strange is quickly terminated.

And I ask if this is what Jesus of Nazareth began. Was he not supremely open to life in all its untidiness, inconvenience and stubborn vitality? Can the genuine Jesus be found in a Church which is fenced in, groomed and trimmed, its beautiful stained glass screened against itchy-bites, its wide-open doors policed against outcasts by grim vergers and against heretics by theologically-educated clerics?

Rick: After reading your beautiful and palpable description of life in the African bush, I was inspired to tell a story of my own.

During World War II, I spent much of my summers on the farm of an aunt and uncle. It is situated near a tiny village, Vasa, Minnesota, just twelve miles from my home town, Red Wing. Surrounding Vasa are the properties of numerous farmers who were either born in Sweden or were first generation Swedish-Americans. My uncle was born in Sweden as were his siblings. My aunt was born in the US to Swedish immigrants.

Among my most precious memories are those associated with the harvest. Virtually all the farmers in the community worked in concert going from farm to farm to bring in the bounty of the summer. As a young boy I enthusiastically joined the men in the field helping to load shocks of grain on horse-drawn wagons to bring them to the gnashing noisy thresh machine that separated straw from the grain. I witnessed the hard working sweaty, swearing Swedes who toiled with seeming glee over the rewards from the earth. For the most part, they spoke Swedish to one another although all spoke perfect English. I think Jesus would have enjoyed working with this hearty earthy crew.

In the village, the Lutheran Church stands on a promontory, its steeple visible for miles around. It was built by the hands of the early settlers from indigenous materials. In the cemetery that embraces the Church one finds a field of Swedish names on markers, many indicating birth in Sweden in the late 18th and early 19th centuries.

Although prosperity was found it was gained by hard work, sacrifice and endurance. There is no question in my mind that the Church was a fundamental inspiration and consolation to that immigrant community sustaining them in the often hostile foreign environment. I doubt any of those crusty Swedes sought or accepted gratuitous spiritual advice. When one farmer was chided by the pastor for not attending services, he reportedly said, "It is better to be in the field thinking about God than to be in church thinking about my crops." Yet, most were found in the pews on Sunday morning worshiping with utter reverence. I recall no evidence of prejudice or exclusionary behavior amongst them. In short, this remains an enduring example of a highly successful church-community relationship.

Thus, when I read your lament of the Church, citing its exclusiveness, prissiness and pettiness it was depressing to think anyone encounters such a situation. It is foreign to me. That church of the sweaty, swearing Swedes I experienced was celebratory, life-affirming and wholly supportive of the earthy community it served. Obviously, our life situations have much to do in shaping our perceptions of the Church.

Mick: Experiences differ. I hail from a country despoiled by the British, you from one long free of colonialism. You have grown up as it were in the bosom of the Church. I came to it as a young man. You have spent your life in a close, familiar congregation. I spent twenty years in a completely secular life after divorce excluded me from the Eucharist.

I question whether our experience is the main point here. Yes, it may lead us to differing conclusions about the Church, each of us having had different experiences of it at a local level. But the Church at large is the focus at this point.

I imagine it's rather like living in a small, peaceful town in South Africa fifty years ago. Whites kept to themselves and Blacks stayed in their allotted place. Peace reigned, and a degree of mutual respect was the order of the day, surprising though that may seem to some.

But a person in that place had only to look up and see what it was that kept the "peace", and everything else took on a new look.

Similarly, homogeneity of the Church at a local level preserves an appearance of openness. A local culture of White Christians of Western origin in South Africa gets on as well as can be. So also a local culture of Americans of Swedish origin has a degree of harmony and apparent inclusiveness. But whatever happens at a local level in the Church, a Christian has only to lift up his or her eyes to see that the type of person welcomed by Jesus are excluded from its wider fellowship. And all in the name of order, or right doctrine or some other specious reason.

Rick: If I follow you correctly you seem to say that the positive influences and experiences afforded by the local Church are nullified if there is corruption in the leaders of the "larger" Church. That is to say, the emotional and spiritual values offered by local church groups (no matter how illusory you consider them) are nullified because of bad actors at the top. You say, " . . . homogeneity of the Church at the local level preserves the *appearance* (italics mine) of openness." Do you mean that comity between parishioners facilitated by the Church is a sham?

Maintaining peace and mutual respect despite inequities among groups of people is not necessarily a bad thing nor is it hypocritical to create tranquil space for parties to dispassionately discuss their differences. It is better than allowing a sincere and honest outpouring of rage.

I am confident that within every church body there is a "shadow church." The shadow church is made up of those who passionately embrace the idea of a transcendent non-material reality expressed in the rituals and doctrines of their particular affiliation. Yet they cannot subscribe to each and every doctrinal detail but consider that discrepancy tolerable.

Undoubtedly there are rascals in Church hierarchy as there are in all human institutions. I have no cogent recommendations for changing that situation. I do not, however, see why the mission of the Church must be suspended until all is made right.

Mick: Point taken. You accurately describe the Church as it is. I'm part of this hybrid creature. You are quite correct that, like every other human institution, it is not homogenous. And, like the curate's egg, it's good in parts. It can't simply stop in its tracks—but it can repent.

We are here discussing inclusiveness. I make my point again briefly. Jesus went before us. He shattered both Jewish and Roman norms of taking in good people and excluding the bad. We are Christians in response to him.

So what justifies exclusion? Not baptized? You can't receive communion at the Lord's Supper. Not sexually straight? You can't be a bishop. Don't believe in the resurrection? You are not Christian. Don't obey the Pope? You're not a proper church. Don't speak in tongues? You're not saved. A Muslim? Go to your mosque.

I could recite instance after instance where we put God's children beyond the pale.

Solutions for next Sunday? Open our church's doors wide to anyone and everyone. Sit next to the smelly, mad street lady. Watch masculine gay men kiss and then receive the bread and wine. Vote for a lesbian to be bishop because she's the best person for the job. Welcome the scared pedophile with open arms, deep understanding and massive support. Rejoice in racial and cultural difference. Invite our Muslim neighbor to share every aspect of our fellowship. Go to the Buddhist for guidance in meditation and spirituality. Be poor to give to the poor.

But there is a problem: All these people recognize at a deep emotional level that many Christians—and I'm one of them—preach one thing and do another. "Go into the highways and byways—but don't bring anyone in here who doesn't meet our standards." So they're not likely to darken our doorway.

Rick: The discussion of inclusiveness inevitably involves a discussion of *prejudice.* In this context I define prejudice as pre-judging, making quick evaluations with meager and incomplete information. Prejudice is a primitive, normal human defense mechanism analogous to our biologic immune systems. Prejudice is instinctively aroused by confrontation with new and potentially threatening situations that may cause an alteration of the *status quo* (homeostasis in biologic systems). If the reaction of the immune system is inappropriate or excessive, great harm may result. Similarly, if prejudice is unenlightened and extreme, we all know what that can do to interpersonal relationships and society at large.

Encountering an unshaven, staggering male in a dark alley will probably cause fear and avoidance. A more critical evaluation may disclose a homeless diabetic who desperately needs medical attention. We should all automatically inspect our prejudices for their authenticity. When more information is gained, our actions precipitated by our prejudice, can be modified or completely overridden.

Members of a church live in two worlds, one of the spiritual, the other of civil society. Each world has its own set of rules that may be congruent or divergent. These rules are established to maintain the stability and integrity of each community. The rules can be changed but it is natural for institutions and people to prefer gradualism and conservatism to avoid chaos and the inconvenient or unnecessary disruption of their missions.

Some rules may not be amenable to change in the eyes of many if not most of the constituents. I doubt many with common sense would deliberately invite a murderer-rapist into the parlor of his home with his daughters and wife. Nor do I think the victims and parents of victims of pedophilia have an obligation to shield the perpetrators from the consequences of civil or ecclesiastical sanctions. Our freedoms are often pre-empted by the rules of society and the church. It cannot be avoided.

We must all be aware of our prejudices and reflexively analyze each one for their authenticity and potential for harm. Where they are pernicious, redress and change may be necessary for the good of society and the church. Such change, however, ought to be sought with patience and civility if it is to be effective and enduring.

10

Decadence

T he wealthy West is often accused by poorer nations—and many of its own people—of decadence. Its root-and-branch decay will one day bring about its downfall, it is said.

Rick: Fifty years ago my alma mater offered a semester course in philosophy entitled, *The Disintegrating Sensate Society*. Discussion developed around an analysis of a number of books including *Darkness at Noon* by Arthur Koestler and *A Portrait of the Artist as a Young Man* by James Joyce. The thesis was developed that Western society was in decline because of an obsession with materialism in all its manifestations.

About a year ago I chanced to meet the professor again who taught the course. I asked him if his predictions had come true or were about to come true. He said unequivocally, "Yes." Since he instigated the course one might question his objectivity. Nonetheless, his ideas reflect a widely-held view that the West, child of the Enlightenment, is indeed in a state of *decadence*.

Empires, nations, tribes and societies decline for many reasons that are often difficult to pinpoint. In other cases, from an historical perspective, the seeds of decadence are apparent such as demographics, economic failure, over-population, inadequate food supplies, invading hordes, pestilence, incompetent governance, corruption and the like.

Often the reasons for decline are not apparent to the leaders of a particular society or group and, therefore, no corrective measures are or can be taken. Mick, my questions are: Do you agree that Western society is decadent? If so, what are the chief factors responsible for the decline? Is materialism one? What if anything can be done to ameliorate the decay?

Mick: I find myself hesitating in response to your questions. I'll try to explain why. When I was a boy, Euro-Africans in Southern Africa almost always employed servants. They had the comparative wealth to do so.

A man servant who once worked for my family came from Malawi. He had migrated 600 kilometers south to earn a few dollars a day. This was better than a few dollars a month at home. Like most of his race and time, he had no shoes. As a result his feet were heavily calloused—but not enough to resist the sharpest thorns. I recall one day watching him digging just such a thorn out of his foot with considerable discomfort. The next payday he appeared with new sandals, fashioned out of a discarded motor car tire by a local entrepreneur.

The point I'm making is that the poor of the world today would give their back teeth to become "decadent" and "materialistic" like the West. What poverty-stricken nation or group would not, I wonder? Perhaps we should acknowledge that our Western society is just plain successful.

Rick: Your point is well taken. Poverty must be an awful thing. Since it was my good fortune to be born at a certain time and certain place I have never known poverty and deprivation. Hence, I can understand it only in the abstract. When a person is starving or has no shelter, he or she is not interested in philosophic discussions. Materialism looks pretty good to any in such situations.

How do societies or individuals extricate themselves from poverty? Can or should they themselves be the main engines of their release? Or must aid come from societies that have material wealth? These are age old questions without pat answers. If the wealthy Western materialist societies are to be of assistance, they must have strength and solvency. This brings us back to the original question about a decadent West.

You are right in saying that Western society has been successful. I doubt there have been any societies in history that have provided more people with material well being. You may not agree that there is any evidence of decadence at all.

I have made a list of what I believe may serve as criteria or tests for decadence in civil society.

1. Instability of the family.
2. Rising crime.
3. Decline of the arts and cultural institutions.
4. Public moral apathy.
5. Public and private gluttony, over-consumption and depletion of natural resources.
6. Economic instability with unsustainable private and public debt.

I am sure others could be listed. From my perspective I see evidence for decadence in all of the categories. Maybe I am naïve and should know better that there have been cycles in human society when all of the above and more were rampaging about. Yet humankind seems to have a resilience to survive the worst calamities. Maybe the forces of entropy that periodically dissolve societies are too strong to influence. What do you think?

Mick: "Things ain't what they used to be," is a common refrain of ancient codgers like us. I remind myself that my parents were brought up nearly a century ago, and I was formed in the 1940s and 1950s. So I mustn't be surprised if I find some aspects of life either unfamiliar or downright unpleasant in this time of rapid change.

What I'm trying to say is that decadence may be a matter of perspective. This is not to deny that Western cultures are to a degree decadent. But isn't it possible that the instances you list are symptoms and not the illness?

If I try to identify an underlying malady, it may be that Western decadence is symptomatic of a failure to change. A society (or a Church) which responds incorrectly to a changed environment tends to lose its mettle. The Hebrew Bible is full of stories about God's people failing to hear and heed God's messages. The prophets proclaimed this failure and called for changed behaviors.

So rather than ask, "Are we decadent?" I prefer to wonder, "What part of God's message are we refusing to respond to?"

Rick: Indeed, my six points represent symptoms. A physician constructs what is called a differential diagnosis based on symptoms and signs observed.

Ultimately and hopefully, this will lead to a diagnosis of a specific disease. This is very important so that a specific treatment can be applied. I frequently gave non-specific or "symptomatic" treatment to make a patient more comfortable. I never felt entirely comfortable doing this until I made a specific diagnosis because I knew the underlying disease was not being treated.

Perhaps the most important point in the diagnostic algorithm is elucidation of the cause. Unfortunately, many diseases continue to be "idiopathic" or of unknown cause making specific treatment impossible. Most cancers fall into this category

Continuing with the medical metaphor and the case at hand, our patient is civil society (humankind). The diagnosis is *decadence*. What is the cause? You have suggested it may be due to a failure to respond appropriately to a changed environment. In addition you have postulated a failure of response to "God's message," as a possible cause.

Can you elaborate on the failures of adapting to change? Moreover, explain how one who does not believe in a non-material reality can invoke the precepts of God?

Mick: Again, response is not easy because it involves treading a tightrope over an abyss. Below are the sharp rocks of Church prohibitions about heresy, and around them boil fierce currents of censure.

First, you are right to talk of "precepts"—that is, of commands or principles governing action. Second, a precept by definition derives from an authority. But what authority gives us our precepts, and how?

I'm saying that we have two basic choices. We can suppose that our universe is an "accident", the outcome of fortuitous circumstances. Or we can suppose that it is purposeful and therefore derives from someone (to use a metaphor).

I prefer the latter. You might say that I have bet my life's shirt on the universe as a purposeful creation rather than a happenstance.

But I think that the creation is itself the message. The cause of a cancer may be unknown. But I have faith that a cause exists. That's the way the world works. That's the creator's message. So the symptoms we call "decay-dence" are God's wake-up call. "Change! Or you will decay and self-destruct. That's how my world works," says God to us all.

Rick: We are in agreement in that we *choose* to believe the universe is creation rather than happenstance. We can't prove the proposition but we intuit it. This belief provides a basis for understanding how the world works. This discussion centers on morality. I would like to paraphrase a biblical injunction:

> If we say we have no moral imperfections we deceive ourselves and the truth is not in us.

Consciousness imposes morality on humankind. Animals create no offenses among themselves because I doubt they are able to reflect on their actions. If there is no awareness there is no offense. Decadence is meaningful only to conscious humankind. There are those who are aware of their offenses but do not care and are morally numb. Others perceive and accept the reality of their shortcomings and make efforts to redress the wrong. Yet others never become aware of their moral failure and though they cause offense no redress is possible.

Thus, I see consciousness as the root of decadence. But, if there is any hope of achieving a morally perfect world it will be consciousness that enables us to find the way. It is a two-edged sword. Until the perfect world is realized there will be ebbs and flows, successes and failures as is well documented in human history. Due to our fundamental natures, success may never be reached. In the meantime we must live in the world as it is and attempt to make the best accommodation possible.

For some, Jesus of Nazareth provides the road map and heightens our moral acuity. For others, Jesus the Christ is the guide. Do you think the distinction between the Nazarene and the Christ is of any consequence?

Mick: I think you're correct about human capacity for self-reflection being at the root of all morality. The existence of a self-reflective being creates a moral imperative.

Working out "the best accommodation possible" at the social level has proved to be a long process so far. Witness the many and varied attempts over the ages to do that. Witness also the struggles of each of us to work out our best accommodation in daily life.

I take it you are wondering if I think that Jesus laid down imperatives for us. There are two parts to my tentative response.

First, I think we now know more about the Jesus of history than anyone before us except those who knew him personally.

Second, another response is to accept the Church's vision of Jesus as the Messiah ("Christ" in Greek). But if I do that, I have to also buy into a pre-modern world-view, upon which all traditional teachings depend.

I choose the first option. If I perceive Jesus as my forerunner in history, then I can affirm in my life the paths he took. I do that by making my own paths, in my own way, just as settlers create new cultures from the foundations laid by their pioneers.

The history of Jesus contains the seeds of the good life. The world is much more than just those seeds. But the whole fails to attain its potential without them.

I suppose my thesis is that decadence inevitably results if we don't carry forward what Jesus gave us about the way God does things—which the gospels term "the kingdom of God".

11

Damnation

An ancient tradition of the Christian Church is that certain people, ultimately known only to God, go to hell. Once there, so it is said, they are tormented eternally to punish them for the evil they have done while alive.

Mick: Flavius Josephus was born soon after Jesus died. His knowledge of Palestine was considerable. He knew of Jesus and John the Baptist, mentioning that "the tribe of Christians, so called after him [Jesus], has still to this day not disappeared".

I was startled recently by Josephus' *Discourse Concerning Hades*, written about the same time as the gospels. For there in all its sordid glory is the Church's vision of Hell. Get the reek of brimstone from this excerpt:

> To these [the damned] belong the unquenchable fire, and that without end. A certain fiery worm, never dying, continues its eruption out of the body with never-ceasing grief . . .

Westerners don't like this idea of hell, living as they do in tolerant and relatively kindly societies. I'm interested in your approach, Rick. Do you think damnation to hell is the fate of unrepentant sinners?

Rick: As a sports fan, particularly of American football and baseball, I am acutely aware of the necessity of umpires to judge infractions of the rules of the respective games. Without the assessment of penalties, the games would be chaotic and dysfunctional. So it is with life. Everyone seeks justice. Frequently, infractions go undetected or are inappropriately assessed. What then? No justice is done. Life isn't fair.

In Western civil law there are so-called *statutes of limitation*. These terminate claims for justice after a prescribed interval from the point of the offence to the claim for justice. The length of the interval is based on the nature and seriousness of the infraction. It is short if it is trivial. It is long or indefinite for crimes that are serious such as those committed by the Nazis.

Does death define the statute of limitations for human wrongdoing? If one believes in God and divine justice, the answer is, no. "Vengeance is mine, I will repay, says the Lord." Finally, it is God who administers justice, if not during our earthly journeys, then certainly in what lies beyond.

What form the justice of God will take I have no idea. As for Josephus' vision of Hell and punishment, it was undoubtedly derived from the prevailing imagery of his cataclysmic times. He may have, unwittingly, described his own punishment as he was hardly a shining example of virtue.

Mick: I have difficulties with your position so far.

First, if you're correct, then surely one good reason for going straight would be fear? I can understand someone who remains a dedicated Christian at least partly for this reason, but it doesn't seem the most worthy of motives.

Second, is it valid to use human legal processes as more than a useful metaphor? I had hoped that God is other than a judge who repays regardless. My understanding is that the ancient "Vengeance is mine . . ." has been superseded by another metaphor—the loving and forgiving father.

Indeed, I had supposed that the central message of Jesus was that opinions of his time about judgment were misguided. If this is not the case, I don't understand what's unique about being Christian. Condemning sinners to damnation is easy. Forgiving them is not. Being a sinner, I know which I prefer.

Rick: I think you are right that Jesus greatly softened the idea of vengeance and retribution as was understood in the Old Testament. He emphasized love and forgiveness over condemnation. In this context my thoughts go back to Martin Luther and the times in which he lived. Then there were monsters abroad ready to devour the sinner causing much fear in Christians. Release was to be bought with money or good deeds. Then a light went on in Luther's head. The New Testament and in particular the writings of Paul said that we are saved from the consequences of our offences by grace and faith in Jesus. If one believes in Jesus Christ and accepts his message then there should be no fear of damnation.

Allow me to briefly extend my previous sports metaphor. I love playing golf. In many ways golf reflects life experiences. It is full of challenges and great rewards. It can also be a source of disappointment and occasional penalties. I do not dwell on the penalties but try harder to avoid them when possible. The total experience is delight. It is not the threat of penalty that motivates me. It is the sheer joy of the game that engages me.

Of course my reference to earthly jurisprudence is a metaphor. You and I as sinners need to be reminded of our moral frailties and the possible consequences of them. We should not, however, be paralyzed by negative thoughts of damnation. Rather, we should be energized by the positive example of Jesus who wants us to have life abundantly. What the ultimate justice of God will entail I do not have the hubris to speculate upon.

Mick: It's the very idea of conditional love that I don't like. That is, I will care for you as long as you . . . And if you don't then . . .

But don't get me wrong. I accept what you say about eternal risk assessment. If a person acknowledges that he or she sins then the possibility of eternal punishment will usually lead to considering alternatives. Bernard Shaw (I think) once said something like, "The prospect of being hung the next morning sharpens the mind wonderfully".

Martin Luther may have been correct. Though it should be noted that apart from getting terribly constipated, he didn't like peasants upsetting the social order of the day by fighting oppression. And his hatred of Jews isn't now acceptable. But, like the threat of eternal damnation, those were things of his time.

As for metaphors, they are all we have when we consider God. The deity is by definition beyond description. To all intents and purposes God *is* a metaphor. So why not God as completely loving and forgiving?

If you want corrective therapy, how about it having been written into the way the universe works? In other words, we are all visited by the consequences of our actions. My shoulder aches on cold days *because* I tried to bowl fast at cricket even though I knew I shouldn't (*hubris*). My marriage broke up *because* . . . and so on. Though why I should always have been too poor to play golf isn't immediately apparent to me.

Rick: The traditional, classic Protestantism, in which I was raised and to which I adhere to this day says that the love of God as manifested in Jesus Christ is unconditional except that you must believe in him. This is the only condition as I see it.

Luther lived in different times. I will not defend him in this forum except to say his positive contributions outweigh his human failures. He radically changed the course of not only Christianity but of Western society as well.

As for metaphors of God I am sure there are as many as there are people who believe in a supreme being. Within groups that associate because of this common belief there are some common features. Citing again the traditions of classic Protestantism, God is a personal God who is interested in me as an individual. If God is all powerful, this power is not only manifested in the macrocosm but also in the microcosms where ordinary people dwell. In my book that's the way the universe works.

Mick: I once rested comfortably with your conclusion that non-belief is the only qualifier which could lead to damnation. But when I tried practicing acceptance of others, my position changed. I found that unconditional acceptance can't be qualified.

What I mean is that you are the only you I have. If you must change before I can relate to you, how can you trust me? For if I don't accept you for who you are, sooner or later I will demand that you become the person I want you to be. In doing so I diminish you. That I have no right to do. For if I have such a right, don't others have the same right over me? We are not here to diminish each other, but to build each other up in order to become what God meant us to be—or as close as possible to that, given our weaknesses and sins.

Unconditional acceptance of you doesn't mean, however, that I must approve of or condone your bad behavior. (Yes, defining what makes an action "bad" presents great difficulties—but that must be dealt with another time.) Acceptance does mean that I will either change my position or negotiate a change of your behavior. But I will *not* reject you if either you or I cannot change. For acceptance is driven by goodwill, and goodwill by charity, and only charity prevails in the end.

That, if you like, is my metaphor for God's unconditional acceptance.

I take it that by "belief" you don't mean wholehearted assent to spoken or written propositions. That approach has too many holes in it to stand. So perhaps you mean by belief an attitude to life which is marked by commitment despite the risk of being utterly, disastrously wrong. If "belief" is betting one's shirt on a poor man who got himself killed two thousand years ago, then I'm with you.

Finally, I remind myself that Jesus doesn't seem to have judged others. So I refuse to say that those who don't take a bet on Jesus are going to be damned. God belongs to everyone, appearing to us in many forms, in many metaphors. The stand taken by Jesus is epitomized by his metaphor of a loving father, which we know as the Parable of the Prodigal Son. That's what I bet my shirt on.

Rick: Our interpersonal relationships are continuously evaluated by each party for quality and content. That is how we decide who we want as friends, associates or spouses. Unfortunately, it does not always work out. When one of the parties is judgmental and attempts to control or change the other party to satisfy his or her particular prejudices, a formula for discord and general trouble is created. Often the judgmental individual is unwilling to accept reciprocal judgment.

Jesus said it well: "Why do you see the speck that is in your brother's eye, but do not notice the log that is in your own eye?" Passing judgment on others is risky business. We may dislike certain people and not want to associate with them but we ought not to stand in judgment of them. Rather we should try to treat everyone with respect, understanding and good will. I know this is easier said than done. For guidance, Mick, I "believe" in the man called Jesus. In this we completely agree.

12

Theology

O nce called the "Queen of Sciences", theology has increasingly taken an intellectual back seat in Western academia. The number of scholars devoting their lives to the subject has diminished to a comparative trickle.

Mick: It's usual to start a discussion of theology by pointing out that the word derives from two Greek words: *theos* (God) and *logos* (word). In other words, theology is discourse about God just as biology is about *bios* (living things).

It's much less usual to go to the heart of the matter and point out that the word "God" is essentially empty of meaning. Christians universally acknowledge that God is "that which is utterly other than ourselves", the Unknown, the Absolute.

So when you or I talk about God we have no referent to attach to the word other than "that which cannot be known". Jesus himself acknowledged this when he used the image of a father to talk of God. In contrast, to take one example, the word "cat" has many millions of living entities as its referent.

Bishop Richard Holloway uses an analogy. Let's suppose, he says, that I have a map of a particular country or region. Before going there I can get a good idea of the lay of the land by studying the map. I will see that if I go northwards out of a certain town, I will see on my left a lake and a range of mountains ahead. And I will know that the next village lies about ten kilometers away.

To verify the accuracy of the map I have only to visit the country which it portrays.

Similarly, books on human physiology provide verbal and diagrammatic maps of the human body. A trainee doctor will have some idea of the human heart well before the first anatomy practical. Actual dissection of a human corpse will show how good the abstract description was.

But what about theology? It is supposed to be a verbal map of God, in the same way as an anatomy textbook is a verbal map of the human body. But in fact it proves to be something like a map of a country which doesn't exist. We can argue as much as we like about this or that aspect of theology. But there is no real country or body to refer to. God is absolutely other than us.

Theology turns out to be an artificial construct. In effect, therefore, when we do theology our discourse is about how we are filling the empty word "God". So to say, "God is good" is actually to propose that human beings define God that way, not to say anything about God. Theology is the ultimate form of navel-gazing.

The tragedy is that to this day people abuse and kill each other over theological rights and wrongs which cannot in any sense be verified.

Rick: Similar to most people I enjoy beauty. In particular I am enthralled by poetry and classical music from the romantic period. However, often what I consider beautiful is ugly in other eyes or ears. Actually, I have never seen nor heard beauty. Rather I have seen and heard the vehicles upon which beauty rides. I also have a sense in my mind of what beauty is.

People of knowledge and taste have disagreements about what constitutes universal exemplars of beauty. Despite the lack of concrete referents the subject of beauty has and will always be a subject of discussion and writing.

There is a great body of knowledge or information that is conceptual and abstract, wholly unverifiable by materialist standards. This knowledge resides entirely in the mind. It could well be that this abstract body of knowledge exceeds that of the physical universe. To apportion that is a worthless task.

So it is with God. I know many people to whom the word God is pregnant with meaning. They would disagree that God is the unknown and unknowable.

However ridiculous their images of God may be to some observers, those images are real to them. I would think everyone is entitled to think of God as he or she wishes.

In this sense I am not disturbed there is a discipline called *theology*. In fact I take great pleasure in reading theology. Theology often yields new insights into life and human struggles and successes throughout history.

Of course theology is a human construct. I don't know what other kinds of constructs there can be. Humans can say "God is good" and many other things. Who but humans can describe or characterize God? If God exists and chooses to make himself known, who will recognize his presence? Certainly it will not be the apes or other animals. As far as I know, humans are the only animate beings on earth who have the consciousness and mental capacity to conceptualize the idea of God and to exchange information about their ideas concerning Him. In other words, *theology* is virtually inevitable and unavoidable.

I am in accord that it is a tragedy that people abuse and kill others over some theological principle or dogma. At the same time I am not optimistic that the elimination or disregard of theology will play much of a role in cleansing the world of its problems. I see no harm in letting theology evolve and try to perfect the world as no other disciplines or institutions have been able to do to this point in time.

Mick: Your comparison of theology with beauty is an excellent one. Beauty is in the eye of the beholder. Each of us has our personal and individual construct of it.

I've noticed, for example, that few share my opinion that snakes are beautiful. On my part, I usually can't see beauty in spiders. Similarly, art may be thought beautiful by one generation and not by another. Theology also has its shifting and changing fashions over successive generations.

However, let's not fail to notice that both art and theology each has an enduring core spanning not only generations, but millennia. Something in us humans seems to recognize that core.

Beauty lingers in Egyptian hieroglyphs and even in the fearsome carvings of blood-soaked Mayan civilizations. Roman and Greek sculptures from the dawn of history still stop most people in their tracks. The best of medieval painting, even though darkened by centuries, continue to stir our emotions.

What is the enduring core of theology?

Let me say first what it is *not*. It is not doctrine. Teaching *about* God is essentially static—one might say lifeless. Doctrine is pseudo-theology because it is formulaic and therefore fossilized. Thinking of doctrine as theology is an ongoing error of many Christians.

True theology, in contrast, engages life's great questions. It is done by every living person. When we concern ourselves with the ultimate, we are all theologians. And because theology is lived out and not just written out, it mutates and changes. It cannot be static.

So there are no final theological answers. The only theological finality is each individual's search for the ultimate, since every experience is always in some sense an end point. Yet each experience, though unique, always leads to another. Lived-out theology therefore always grows.

Rick: I picture our theology as an ancient grape vine, planted 4 000 years ago by Abraham. Today its roots and central stem contain the history of generations of evolving understanding of monotheism. There is evidence of conflict and disagreement and there are broad variations of interpretation of scripture. All this and more is contained within the gnarled stem that every spring gives rise to tender shoots. These shoots in turn bear the grapes from which the new wine of theology is vintaged.

I agree that every person can and should be a theologian. Each believer should come to his own understanding of a unique relationship to God. This may or may not find resonance with an organized church body.

In tracing beliefs of 4 000 years ago and comparing them with the present, it is sometimes hard to believe Christianity came from the same ancient stem of the vine. Yet, there is no question but it did. The common core coursing through the vine from ancient times is the love of God and reverence for Him. This is immutable. This is bed rock from which all branches originate. There *are* some things written in stone.

Mick: I'm not quite sure what to make of your grapevine analogy. It is most graphic and illustrates a great truth—namely, that the essence of each of us is derived from what has gone before.

Genetically, we are the fruit of those few ancestors whose offspring has survived the rigors of God's creation. Culturally, we are similarly imprinted with thousands of years of social wisdom and learning.

Likewise, Christian theology derives from many generations of those for whom Jesus of Nazareth has been the pioneer upon whom they have based their ways of life. Our theological roots in the West go back to the dawn of time—far beyond our religious ancestors, the Hebrews and Greeks.

My thesis (not an original one) is based upon the idea, which I first encountered in the writings of Lloyd Geering, that it is possible to observe certain radical change-points in the "history of God"—and therefore in the history of theology. If the resulting "axial ages" are taken into account, your grapevine and bedrock analogies seem to break down.

The idea is that one such radical change happened when humanity conceived the idea that "God is one" and not many. At that point an axial age ended. The axial age of monotheism has now ended. It is increasingly difficult for humans to revere a personal deity who, when necessary, intervenes in nature.

Our theology must change accordingly. It is as though the branches, leaves and fruit of the vine have wilted. We can now have wine only if we graft a completely new plant onto the ancient roots. The enlivening sap will still flow from the soil, for that is how things work. But the vine itself will look utterly different from its predecessor.

To sum up: Theology is alive and well as long as debate goes on. It dies as soon as anyone lays down a final, unalterable bedrock of absolute truth. At that point, theology becomes merely a shifting of pieces around a mental chessboard.

13

Schism

Rick: Disagreement occurs in every sphere of human life. Disagreement may cause discord that in turn may lead to dissolution of relationships. As an American the first example that comes to my mind is our Revolution that separated us politically from Great Britain.

Loyalists argued that our differences could be overcome by rational discourse. Others felt the only solution was complete and final separation. The fundamental disagreements between the Colonies and the Crown were so serious and profound that no *modus vivendi* was possible.

It was the extreme of sword and gun that would be the final arbiter. Today I think that few would argue the separation was not ultimately favorable for both parties.

The Church has not been immune from doctrinal disputes that have occasionally resulted in schism. Witness the break between the Greek and Latin Churches in the eleventh century and the Protestant Reformation. Currently, large church bodies are in turmoil over social and doctrinal issues that create potential schisms. Church officials struggle to maintain comity between factions when the disagreements are so deep and fundamental that this observer considers them unbridgeable.

Mick, my question is, why don't these factions simply divorce and establish new churches? It seems to me both sides would be happier and more effective in their respective missions.

Mick: I think one answer to your question concerns the concept of orthodoxy. My point is that perhaps schism arises out of a false concept of the teaching and life of Jesus. God belongs to all. Christians are those for whom Jesus is a prime inspiration.

If a Christian group asserts that affirmation of certain doctrines is a condition of membership then it is duty bound to insist that all its members publicly affirm those teachings. And if anyone strays from the party line, that person must either conform or be cast out. This is the position of the Roman Catholic and Orthodox churches.

Some admit the possibility that group teachings are not absolutely definitive. In that case, orthodoxy is more difficult to enforce. This is pretty much the stand of so-called "Protestant" or "Reformed" churches.

But both insist that their members affirm certain teachings as a condition of continued membership. They also insist that members conform to certain behavioral norms. Expulsion may result from disobedience in either sense. And any group which will do neither is expected to leave.

A dissident group may decide to leave its parent body because it is coming under intolerable pressure from authority or fellow Christians. More often, I suppose, such groups go into schism because they have accepted and internalized the proposition that Christians who perceive the world differently can't remain in fellowship.

Was not a pivotal point of Jesus' life and teaching precisely that we are all acceptable to God? If he's correct, then one can't properly cast out of a fellowship those whom God accepts. Nor is there any point in choosing schism if all are accepted by God.

I don't feel entirely certain about my argument up to this point. I wonder if you can bring more clarity.

Rick: It is common for social organizations to generate what might be broadly called, *mission statements.* Among other things, these statements include reasons for their existence, an enumeration of principles and goals, rules for the conduct of its members and qualifications for membership.

These mission statements give public form and character to the respective organization. In addition, the statements give forewarning to prospective members about what they are signing on to.

All who finally join a specific organization do not necessarily subscribe to every point of the mission statement but join because they believe, on balance, the overall mission corresponds with their aspirations.

In the case of churches, mission statements are usually referred to as *doctrine* that prescribes *orthodoxy* that is often the cause of schism. Dissidents bridle at what they perceive as coercion and loss of free agency imposed by orthodoxy. In response they develop their own orthodoxies.

Dissident orthodoxy is usually more simple than traditional church orthodoxy. Perhaps they have only a few conditions for joining their fellowship, one being acceptance of Jesus as the prime inspiration for life. I doubt anyone who does not subscribe to this idea would be admitted.

Mick, you said, . . "that perhaps schism arises out of a *false concept* of the teaching and life of Jesus." This would imply a claim for truth on your part and error or corruption on the other side. This stance is as doctrinaire as that of the traditional church. Although your doctrine is less complex it is not isolated from the possibility of personal bias and interpretation. By what standard can you claim to have truth and the traditional church is in error?

Mick: I take your point—though perhaps you should give me credit for the word "perhaps". I hope that my personal position in relation to Jesus is supported by reasoned evidence. The difference between what I try to espouse and the orthodoxy of the Church at large is twofold:

1. Even though I may state my position as clearly and as assertively as I can, I do not maintain that I have final answers. And even though I try to live my life on the basis of what I arrive at as "the truth", I recognize that this truth is always provisional. Nothing I adopt is immune to change.
2. Because I think truth is never absolute, I must allow others to differ from me—even though they are part of a fellowship to which I belong. Unity is not achieved through uniformity. I have concluded (though

I may be wrong in this) that Jesus lived and taught acceptance of human difference.

In short, I can at this point see no reason why anyone should be excluded from the fellowship of the Church. It is *not* a club. Though it may adopt an institutional form, no particular form is of its essence. If I'm on the right track, then both the schismatic *and* the Church fail to recognize the generous inclusiveness of Jesus' outlook.

Rick: One of the sources of schismatic force is the very issue of *provisional truth* you raise. I must press you a bit on this. If the universe is a unity and all principles of it are constant how then can *truth* be provisional? It is either truth or it is not.

Let me cite a brief analogy involving clothing. The animal skins primitive man used to warm and protect themselves from the environment look radically different from our modern apparel but the function is exactly the same. There are general principles involved that are universal and immutable namely the function of protecting the person in the case cited. Clothing looks different from age to age but the *truth* of its function is constant.

I have asserted in our previous debates there are bed rock moral principles. They are often difficult to apply with clarity to all current moral dilemmas. Nonetheless we should look critically for the enduring universal and often subtle principles involved.

There are large constituencies on either side of this question. I consider it unlikely that *rapprochement* will ever be reached. As much as I value the idea of unity and comity within the Church, I think schism can be a healing process as I suggested in the introduction to this debate. I see no good reason not to establish a church that prescribes no creed, that espouses no doctrine and demands no orthodoxy. Wouldn't that be a good solution?

Mick: The Church you suggest tongue-in-cheek would have one merit—it would include everyone in whose lives Jesus of Nazareth is central. This is the most fundamental allegiance any Christian can ask or give.

The point I make is this: Even if a group sets up certain norms of conviction and conduct, all it can ever have is verbal assent to propositions. A person can say something a thousand times without that making a whit of difference to his or her behavior. So why have a creed? Why set up doctrines to which people must assent? Why insist on statements of orthodoxy? It doesn't make sense to me.

Or rather, it makes sense only if those who set themselves up (or are set up) as judges of who has stepped outside theological or behavioral boundaries are, wittingly or not, engaged in controlling others.

This is fine if one belongs to the club of those who go to church, recite creeds, believe certain teachings, and follow certain absolute moral principles. But think of the implications even of that. For if it is wrong to *say* something, then it must be wrong to *think* it. Thought-police are just around the corner. Witness the recent attempts in the Church of England to muzzle theological dissent. Witness also the centuries-old counsel of the Roman Catholic Church concerning unholy thoughts.

Who is to say that *any* decision to behave in a certain way is wrong according to "bedrock moral principles"? For what reason? If a moral choice is made for a reason, doesn't it follow that there might be other reasons which lead to entirely another moral choice? If that is possible, then there can be no absolute. Absolutes exclude alternatives.

Doesn't this absolute approach confine moral choice to a straightjacket? Indeed, doesn't it jettison moral choice altogether? For if I know without doubt that something is wrong, I *must not* choose it. I *may* choose it. But I do so knowing that I do "wrong". I suggest that truly mature choice happens only when I *don't* know what is right, when there is no moral absolute. I may have well-tested guidelines. And I may be foolish to ignore them. But only when I work it out for myself can I be said to be truly human.

This of course requires that what I live my life by must always be provisional. It *doesn't* mean that I have no principles or fundamental assumptions guiding my life. Nor does it mean that I may not sometimes have to operate according to those principles without thinking things through—just as when I jump without thinking from the 'bus that's about to run me over. Nor does it mean that I may not have to defend my principles with my life or—more challenging still—with the lives of others.

I hold (provisionally) that principles, even when espoused by people with great authority and rhetorical powers, remain assumptions, to be changed or even discarded when the facts or the situation demonstrate that they no longer apply. And if our principles are provisional then chasing away those whose principles differ will not do. There is no point in schism.

Let me propose a test: Arrange for all your elders, or ministers, or bishops to assemble in one room together. Then ask each in turn, out of the hearing the others, to give a five-minute talk on "The Essence of the Holy Trinity". My hypothesis is that the resulting monologues will bear little resemblance to each other—so little that it would be impossible to put together from them a coherent "doctrine" upon which to base the action of ejecting a heretic or moral renegade from the fellowship of the friends of Jesus.

The Church's greatest sin today is the willful exclusion from its hallowed halls of God's children, and the brothers and sisters of Jesus. Schism exists only because we've invented it. It is neither necessary nor loving.

14

Mission

Mick: The desire of Christians to convert others to their way of life is, I would say, as fundamental as almost any other aspect of their religion. Jesus is said to have told them to "Go out into the whole world and announce the good news to everyone" (Mark 10.15—though this and other similar exhortations are not what Jesus said, but the teaching of early Christian communities).

The hero of the missionary movement is Paul of Tarsus. Some think that he was in a real sense the founder of the Church—though we now know that his missionary effort was only one small part of the rapid spread of Christianity throughout the Roman Empire.

I am one of those who feel a deep sense of discomfort about "preaching Jesus Christ" (whatever that may mean). I would like others to experience with me the life which I lead in the footsteps of Jesus. And I will try to explain what are the important things I think Jesus lived out and talked about.

And again, I do my best to lead a life which is congruent with that of Jesus. I don't know much about what he did. I know a little more about what he said. I must admit that historical information about him is somewhat slight. So in the final analysis, anyone who is interested in Jesus must be able to see him in me, as it were. And they should be able to confirm the basis for my life through the gospels. But it is primarily my interpretation of Jesus, my living out of a Jesus-like way of life in the modern world, which should be compelling.

To put this another way: It is not what I say which matters, but what I do. If, for example, Jesus lived a simple life as a poor man, then the way I live should aim to do the same as far as possible. I may preach about Jesus suffering on the cross with utter conviction, but if comfort and security are my priorities, I'm like a blaring radio, full of nothingness.

Something in me draws back, for example, from trying to convince Muslims, Buddhists, or Jews that my version of the world is inherently better than theirs. I feel the same reluctance to persuade so-called "secular" people that they should become religious. For I don't have final answers to give. I have only a way of life which is founded on that of a pioneering man who lived two thousand years ago.

Rick: I was born and baptized into the Lutheran Church having roots in the immigrant Swedish Lutheran tradition. That immigrant church had a strong evangelic fervor. Yet, it was my experience, that while the clergy publicly admonished us to "make disciples of all nations", we in the pews took a more passive stance. Maybe that is just being Swedish.

I am not a "born-again" Christian. Since my childhood instruction there is a steady unbroken line of faith to the present. I gave the usual child-like assent to what I was taught. When I reached what I would call my "age of discernment" I still found my faith to be valid and valuable to me. So it is to this day. How unexciting you might say.

It has always been difficult for me to talk to others about my faith let alone convince them to accept it. Undoubtedly this derives from the reticence I observed in the old Swedes I sat with in the pews. I have always kept my faith "close to the vest" as it were.

I am reminded of the story of the arrogant Pharisee and the humble tax collector praying in the temple as recounted in Luke 18. Jesus said of them: "For every one who exalts himself will be humbled, but he who humbles himself will be exalted."

Though this passage does not directly bear on evangelism, it demonstrates how an overt display of piety can be self-serving. Asking others to believe as I do, smacks of the same hubris.

Yet, I am in a quandary. If I value my faith, as indeed I do, I must recognize I am the recipient of the beneficence of others who evangelized me.

When one experiences something good, it is natural to tell others and to share the goodness. My wife, who is a world-class cook, often presses me to taste new things. I am grateful for her culinary evangelism as without it I would have missed a whole world of exciting tastes. Her insistence can still be occasionally irritating.

Thus it is with proclaiming Jesus Christ. If one considers him compelling there is an implicit impulse to share his story with others.

Mick, I subscribe to your low-keyed approach of teaching by example rather than exhortation. Emulating the simple life of Jesus ought to be the thrust of evangelism. Unfortunately, I have not lived such a life nor do I think I can. I live without excess but still require creature comforts and pleasures. Is there any hope for me?

Mick: We seem to share a laid-back approach to our subject, an emphasis on the doing rather than the preaching. Perhaps one way to differentiate would be to say that we're both mission-oriented but neither is sold on evangelism. We want to give and share, but we don't want to hector and harangue.

However, I want to put to you a more far-reaching problem. When we as Christians make contact with those of other faiths or of none, I suspect we tend to operate with a sort of unconscious double standard which affects our interactions negatively.

If we are "modest" Christians like you and I, we may go through the motions of being open and understanding. But lurking underneath is (as you infer) a hidden conviction that ours is the better vision. We claim 20/20 vision while the others see less clearly.

And yet at the very core of our faith is the conviction that Jesus died for *all*, not just Christians. Jesus was a Jew. He was not supposed even to touch certain kinds of people. We know for certain that he absolutely refused to be bound by human barriers. Paul understood this clearly. Even the most basic barriers (slave/free, male/female, Jew/Gentile) are broken down by the pioneering life of Jesus.

I ask this: How is it possible to hold that all-embracing degree of acceptance as the crown of our faith and then go on to pronounce that others must become like us? \Surely we are bound to accept them as they are first, and then go on living our Christian lives?

Rick: Oh how I wish your simple approach of universal acceptance could work and let all humankind live in peace and tranquility. My experience tells me the world, at least in present time, just doesn't work like that.

We live in a perpetual moral dilemma. While we might want to live and let live, others refuse to allow it. When a person or group of persons say you should be killed because of your beliefs, the ideal of non-resistance and acceptance seem naïve and dangerous.

In these turbulent times we are forced to judge the rightness of our moral convictions. We cannot avoid the *hidden conviction* we have a better vision for humanity. How we handle that judgment is key. You and I would not force it on others. But when some ideology actively threatens us, it is necessary to resist lest we be swept away.

Mick: I think we have come to this point before in our debates. To illustrate, let's take a look at the word "ideology". It means something like "an integrated, systematic body of concepts about human life and culture". It seems to me that those who say they are Christian "believers" mean that they subscribe to an ideology.

The point I'm making is that Christianity is not an ideology. It has developed into that over the millennia, but it is essentially a way of life. True, any way of life derives in turn from a way of perceiving the world. But that's the crazy thing about being Christian. The ideology is itself anti-ideology. Christians have subscribed to that from the beginning. Paul made it clear when he wrote in 1 Corinthians 13:

> If I have prophetic powers and understand all mysteries and all knowledge . . . but do not have love, I am nothing.

Love crowns everything for a Christian. We are bound to act lovingly towards those whose actions derive from ideologies different from ours.

Our hidden conviction is that love conquers everything that no ideology is worth giving it up. We don't need to defend ourselves from those whose constructs about the world differ from ours. The person whose God is money can't force us to give our lives to it. The Muslim may force a form of words from our lips, but our inner love can't be touched. We may be persuaded that the Trinitarian formula is a word-game. But that does not necessarily affect our loving actions.

It's on this basis that I say that when we follow in the pioneering steps of Jesus, we are bound to love. Converting others to forms of words or worship is pointless.

Rick: The word *ideology* has taken on an unfortunate pejorative connotation. I think there are good ideologies and bad ones. You are advocating an ideology of *love* to which I subscribe. Our focus here should not be on linguistics but on the means of mission. *Ideology* would be a good topic for a future debate.

However, while you and I prefer a low-keyed approach to mission we must still realize that the very fact of our non-verbal lives declares advocacy of our beliefs. We cannot hide behind a coy shyness or reluctance to intrude on others and say we do not stand for something.

I return to an earlier thought of what one should do if life is threatened by another who disagrees with our beliefs. Should we allow ourselves to be slaughtered without resistance? What if you were the last person on earth who loved? What would be accomplished if you allowed yourself to be eliminated?

It is one thing to aggressively proselytize. That is not my style nor is it yours. It is quite another matter to stand by in helpless passivity while the world crashes about us.

Mick: I think I now see more clearly where we differ. Mission in the usual sense means trying to change (convert) others to Christianity. You and I agree that we don't like to do that, that we prefer our lives to attract others. We also agree that our faith is centrally important to us. We think it's the best thing since sliced bread and we will not stand by passively while the world crumbles. Jesus has brought something to our world which is critical to its future wellbeing.

What I'm trying to say is that I cannot refuse exactly the same attachment for a person of another religion or none. I don't want to discount his or her conclusions about what's important, about the great questions of life. If there is to be dialogue between us, I want it to be on the basis of total mutual acceptance—not with the hidden agenda that my faith is better.

If I grant to another what I claim for myself, then mission in the traditional sense is out.

Meaning

Theologians of many persuasions have remarked that the uniquely rapid pace of recent social change has produced an equally unique crisis. Modern humans are in a real sense existentially rootless in a way their ancestors were not. The challenge is one of accessing ultimate meaning in our lives—or what some would call God. Here Mick and Rick try to understand what is meant by meaning.

Rick: Before embarking on the main discussion I think it is appropriate to be sure we are talking about the same thing. We should establish what we mean by *meaning.*

I don't think we will be discussing the meaning or translation of mere words such as cat, horse or house. I suspect we will be talking about the meaning of *life of the human species*; what is its purpose? Does it have significance in the vast expanse of the universe? Perhaps it would be more accurate to use the term *meaningfulness* in this context if life is to be filled with meaning.

I need your take on what meaning means to you.

Mick: I think I was expecting to discuss "meaning" in the sense that individuals find meaning in their lives. I don't have an answer about the bigger sense of the word—except to say that I suspect that the universe exists for the sake of life. But as a living creature I would think that, wouldn't I?

Rick: Good. We are on the same track. I am not sure the universe exists for life alone. There are forces for life *and* death, for building up and tearing down. The outcomes are frequently dependent on the people who wield and influence these forces.

In order to analyze the process of seeking meaning in life, allow me to present three vignettes.

> A young Swedish girl leaves home and family to seek a better life in America. She will never return. On the advice of her father who feels there is no future for her in Sweden because of dire economic circumstances, she embarks for America. A long and dangerous journey ensues before she reaches the New World. There she finds menial work. Marriage is arranged to another Swedish immigrant and she raises a family. In later years, just before her death at 89 she tells me she could not have endured all the pains and tribulations without her faith in God and Jesus Christ. It was her faith that gave life its meaning.

> A young man, born into poor economic conditions, struggles to better himself. He He works tirelessly to put himself through college. His family has told him he has the capacity to do anything he wishes and they are constantly cheering him on. He is successful. Both he and his family find meaning in his struggle and success.

> Another young man approaches a large gathering of people. In a few minutes he will detonate explosives strapped to his body. By performing this terrible act he will have found meaning for his life. From the start of his quest he has found encouragement from his family and friends. They too will find meaning in his act.

Generalizing from these stories there are the following elements:

1. A conscious person who makes decisions;
2. An encouraging and facilitating family or support group;
3. A challenge for change of the *status quo*;
4. A guiding principle leading to a future goal.

The first three factors are derived from flesh and circumstance. The fourth flows from a metaphysical source such as religion, faith or morality, whatever you would call it.

It is clear that finding *meaning* does not always work out well for the individual or society. Many critics of religion say it is the very fact of faith or having stable guiding principles or ideology that is at the root of the world's social upheavals.

If my analysis is reasonably accurate, I am concerned that in an increasingly secularized world the search for meaning will entail predominantly materialist standards or principles. How much money can I accumulate, who can I beat etc? In the West this phenomenon is increasingly evident.

You may counter that radicalism is fueled by distorted metaphysical principles. That may be. But should the West give up its source of transcendent inspiration that fueled civil and material progress in the first place? I submit that will lead to *ennui* and entropy.

Mick: Your point seems to be that we all naturally seek meaning as significance for our lives. If so, the discussion moves on to the relative value of various meanings. If I understand you correctly, you maintain that secular, materialist meanings such as money or suicide bombing are at best unsatisfactory, at worst bad. Those derived from a "source of transcendent inspiration" are good, particularly when they fuel "civil and material progress".

Boiling it down, you appear to say that my life's meaning is *given* to me. It's not something I *make* for myself. Have I got it right?

Rick: In my analysis of the three vignettes, the first element cited was, "A conscious person who makes decisions." Meaning is not *given*. Rather, meaning is selected from a myriad of choices available to the individual. In that sense one can *make meaning* by making choices.

A few years ago I published a treatise on the nature and implications of *consciousness. (Time and the Mystery of Consciousness*, 2003) I proposed the creation of "cells of consciousness" in each person. The cells are composed of *past, present and future*. For the cell to be whole and effective, each of the three components must be represented. Only animals or non-sentient beings live wholly or mostly in the present. They have a rudimentary sense of the past that conditions their responses to the environment but I doubt they have any sense of the future.

This model is helpful to me in analyzing *meaning*. It suggests that meaning resides in the future as a guiding star or principle that energizes and propels the individual toward a goal. At this juncture, religions that propose a future after death can be decisive in giving meaning to this life because the cell of consciousness is complete even at the point of death.

Thus I see the Christian doctrine of resurrection and life hereafter as a positive contribution to a sense of *meaning* in this life.

Mick: Fair enough. You say that we select meaning from the blooming, buzzing confusion that is life. If we didn't have some sort of meaning—in your words a "guiding star or principle"—then we would be like a compass without a magnetic north. It occurs to me, as an aside, that every north has a south. Does the compass point north, or does it point south?

But back to our subject. I think you are saying that we select meanings to place within our cell of consciousness. What we select in the present enters the "past" part of the cell. We look to the future in our cell of consciousness and take certain parts of its myriad possibilities into our present.

Some would say, however, that we don't really choose as much as we think we do. Even as adults, they would say, we are at the mercy of the tides of fortune and the clusters of stimuli which comprise them. For example, it would seem that we are formed by the culture into which we are born and in which we grow and develop. That might explain why Christianity, resurrection and all, appears to mean little to the majority. How does that strike you? Isn't the larger part of life's meaning given to us?

Rick: A couple of analogies occur to me in response to your question. No doubt we are given the bodies, skin color, social circumstances and a variety of specifications that delimit the scope of our individual choices. However, it is of interest to realize the genome of a chimpanzee has 98% homology with that of humans. The 2% difference is obviously of huge moment in differentiating us from the primates.

Poker players are dealt cards not of their choosing. Yet, by working within their limited possibilities some players may, through their skills, be highly successful.

So it can be in our individual search for meaning in life. Our conscious minds give us the tools to work within our limitations to find meaning. Our freedoms may also lead to misery and meaninglessness.

In my circle of associates and friends, Christianity is of immense importance. Even if Christianity "means little to the majority" as you assert, this possibility in no way detracts from its decisive importance in the lives of many. I don't think my fellow Christians adhere to the faith because of the results of popularity polls.

Mick: I suspect that we are walking roughly along the same compass bearing. I say "suspect" because the terms and images we use tend to be dissimilar. I may have it wrong, but here is a brief summary so far:

- Life meaning can derive from faith, from struggle for success, even from the sacrificial death-dealing of a suicide bomber.
- A meaningful life is best chosen according to a guiding principle. Support from loved ones in the choice and on the journey is a great help.
- The guiding principle matters. Ideology flowing from a metaphysical source such as religion is better than materialist ideology, for example.
- Meaning in a human life is not given but selected from a myriad of future possibilities.

Let me start with the latter point.

Future possibilities exist equally for us all. But the *range* of available possibilities for each of two people—say one in China and one in the USA—are very different. More importantly, the available "metaphysical" ideologies are not the same. And if religion is a social thing, then no range of meaning is invalid.

We choose meanings from given options. But are the options "given" in the sense that they are just there as part of our social and physical environments? Or are they "given" in the sense that a supreme originator has "put" them there with deliberate intent?

That's the big question. It seems to me that Jesus (who is my personal pioneer in such matters) held that there is no final answer to it. He said that "God's people" and the despised "others" of his time and place—the foreigners and the Gentiles—have equal access to the divine and therefore to meaning in life. He spoke as a Jew, of course, and not as a Christian.

I may not like a materialist meaning, but can I caste the first stone?

Rick: You have summarized my arguments accurately. The search for meaning is a universal human drive. Meaning galvanizes the will to realize a goal. That goal may be death and destruction as previously described. It would be better if the goal was to sustain life and make it more abundant for all human kind.

It is apparent that simply finding meaning is not necessarily a positive end in itself. There is good meaning and there is bad. At times it is difficult to decide which is which. We must then look for some standard to make a judgment. You and I rely on the example of Jesus. Where we seem to disagree is whether or not Jesus is the representative and messenger of the "supreme originator."